# Perfect Reading

## & Beautiful Handwriting

---

The Intelligent Parent's
Complete Step-by-Step Program
for Teaching Any Child
How to Read & Write in 60 Days!

---

Caroline Joy Adams

EVERYDAY
EDUCATION

Perfect Reading, Beautiful Handwriting: The Intelligent Parent's Complete Step by Step Program for Teaching Any Child How to Read and Write in 60 Days!

## Other books by Caroline Joy Adams

*An Italic Calligraphy Handbook*

*A Woman of Wisdom: Honoring and Celebrating Who You Are*

*The Power to Write: Seven Keys to Discover Your Writer Within*

© 2015 Everyday Education, LLC

P. O. Box 549

Ashland, Virginia 23005

EverydayEducation.com

Excellence-in-Literature.com

ISBN: 978-1-61322-036-8

Originally published by Adams House Publishers, Inc., 1988

# Foreword

Many years ago, I used *Perfect Reading, Beautiful Handwriting* while teaching my oldest son to read and write. As a new homeschooling mom, I was drawn to the simplicity of the method, and as a former calligrapher, I was delighted to be able to teach from a book in which every page was a model of simple, clear penmanship.

When I went back to purchase another copy for our second son, I was disappointed to learn that it was out of print. I ended up making do with my own handwritten copywork sheets and a few other resources. There are good programs for teaching reading and writing, but I have never found another one with the elegant simplicity of this one-volume book, so I am delighted to be able to bring it back into print. I hope you enjoy using it!

May your students find a lifetime of joy in reading well and writing beautifully.

Ashland, Virginia

Everyday-Education.com and Excellence-in-Literature.com

## Teaching the Lessons

Before you begin, here is an overview of how to teach with this book (more detail in the Teaching Tips chapter). You do not have to do every activity every day—lessons can be taught a few letters, words, or sentences at a time, especially if you are working with a very young student.

- Before beginning each day's lesson, briefly review the previous lesson.
- Introduce the letter or sound being learned.
- For the alphabet, trace the letters in the lesson; then copy.
- For other lessons, practice sounding out word families (at, bat, hat, cat, sat, mat, etc.).
- Practice reading the story.
- Do the model story as copywork; copying letterforms and spacing, and writing each word directly beneath the model.
- Use additional copies of the guidesheets for more practice

### Posture and pen hold

Long ago, children were told to sit up straight with both feet flat on the floor and write with their arm supported by a suitably sized desk or table. Through many years of writing and teaching calligraphy, I have become convinced that this is foundational advice. It is nearly impossible to create beautiful pages of lettering if the arm and hand are not supported, yet free to move. The writing surface should be at an appropriate height for a child—if the table or desktop is at armpit level or too low, writing is uncomfortable and tiring.

Another element of penmanship that is equally important is pen hold. A relaxed tripod grip will permit many hours of comfortable writing and avoid the hand and shoulder pain that accompanies a death grip or fist hold. A handwriting teacher of the early twentieth century describes the hold in this way: "The first finger bends naturally, and rests on top of the holder about one inch from the point of the pen; the thumb rests on the holder nearly opposite the first joint of the first finger, and the third and fourth fingers are bent, touching the paper and forming a movable rest." You may see a descriptive drawing of the tripod hold for right or left hand at www.doingwhatmatters.com/how-to-hold-a-pen-or-pencil/.

### Spacing, slant, rhythm, and size

If you look at the models in this book, you will see that each lower-case letter has the same size and slant, and is spaced at a similar distance from other letters. Copying directly beneath the model helps the student see and practice all these details. I have found that it is also helpful to develop a steady writing rhythm. When I notice that I am writing messily, it is usually because I am rushing and have not established a rhythm. I can instantly transform a scribbly line to neatness and order by taking a deep breath and "marching" the downstrokes as if they are pacing to the beat of a metronome (*down* and up and *down* and . . .). This helps each letter to have the same size, slant, and spacing.

#### Using this book with *Model-Based Writing*

If you are using the Absorb, Consider, Transform, and Create learning sequence taught in *Model-Based Writing* (see ModelBasedWriting.com), you may use the reproducible guide sheets in this book for copying and other writing assignments in MBW.

On the next page, you will find examples of ways to schedule these lessons. The essential thing to remember is that these are *suggested* schedules. Some students will find the lessons fun and easy and want to hurry ahead and do more lessons. Others will struggle and need extra time. Please feel free to adapt the lessons and schedule to your student's needs.

## Scheduling Options

Because you are teaching both reading and writing, do not rush through the book. Although each lesson could possibly be completed by a motivated student in a single day, many students will feel more confident and do better work if they can spend a little more time in practice. Keep in mind Charlotte Mason's admonition that short lessons—10 to 15 minutes at a time—help children stay focused. When attention wanders, retention drops, so brief lessons with complete concentration will accomplish more than a long lesson with wandering focus.

**Suggested schedule for a very young student or one with learning challenges:**

|  | Monday | Tuesday | Wednesday | Thursday | Friday |
|---|---|---|---|---|---|
| Review | 5 minutes | 5 minutes | 5 minutes | 5 minutes | 5 minutes |
| Introduce | x |  |  |  |  |
| Trace |  | x |  |  |  |
| Sound Out |  | x |  |  |  |
| Read |  |  | x | x |  |
| Copy |  |  | x | x |  |
| Practice |  |  |  |  | x |

**For a school age student who is not yet reading:**

|  | Monday | Tuesday | Wednesday | Thursday | Friday |
|---|---|---|---|---|---|
| Review | 5 minutes | 5 minutes | 10 minutes | 5 minutes | 15 minutes |
| Introduce | x |  | x |  |  |
| Trace | x |  | x |  |  |
| Sound Out |  | x |  | x |  |
| Read |  | x |  | x | x |
| Copy |  | x |  | x |  |
| Practice |  |  | x |  | x |

**For a school age student who is already reading:**

|  | Monday | Tuesday | Wednesday | Thursday | Friday |
|---|---|---|---|---|---|
| Review | 5 minutes | 5 minutes | 5 minutes | 5 minutes | 5 minutes |
| Trace letters | x |  | x |  |  |
| Copy | x | x | x | x |  |
| Practice |  | x |  | x | x |

## Make reading an everyday part of life

As you work through this book, you can help your student become a fluent reader by continuing to read aloud. Choose books at a variety of reading levels, from picture books to early readers, chapter books, and poetry. Reading aloud not only helps your students develop important pre-reading skills, it allows them to enjoy stories that are above their reading level and increases knowledge, empathy, and the ability to take a big-picture view of events.

In addition to reading aloud, I also suggest frequent use of professionally recorded audiobooks. A well-performed audiobook is a delight. It brings a story to life, especially for auditory and kinesthetic learners, and can immerse listeners into the setting and events of the book, which helps to whet the appetite for more reading. From a practical perspective, professionally-created audiobooks also provide the correct pronunciation of unfamiliar names and words, and they provide a good model for how to read expressively and well.

### *Reading time*

*One must be drenched in words, literally soaked in them,*
*to have the right ones form themselves into the proper pattern at the right moment.*
Hart Crane

Reading—being saturated with well-crafted words—is an essential prerequisite for writing well, so I recommend implementing personal reading time, as well as reading for school and as a family. If your children see you reading, they will believe you when you tell them that reading is important. I suggest creating a quiet time each day where everyone in the family sits quietly and reads, looks at books, or does a silent paper-based activity such as drawing, journaling, or planning. We usually did this after lunch, and I found it worked best when the boys sat in different spots where they could not see one another, and I sat in the middle where I could see or hear everyone.

If you have not been doing quiet time, you may want to begin with just five or ten minutes and gradually work up to an hour. Young children may fall asleep, which is fine. Quiet time is a peaceful pause in the day, but I found that it is effective only if 1) you participate, and 2) it is a paper-based activity (no screens). If you spend this precious hour in the shallows of social media or run around doing housework, you not only miss the opportunity for creative or spiritual refreshment in the middle of the day, but you also communicate to your children that reading is really not very important. It may be hard at first to make time for it, but I believe you will be glad you did.

—*You will find more articles on reading and the learning lifestyle at DoingWhatMatters.com.*

# Chapter 1.

## About Reading
## About Handwriting
## Tips for Teaching

# About Reading

*Just what is the method of reading instruction used in this hook?*

The "phonic" method is used here, which is the simplest, fastest and most effective way to teach reading. It consists of first teaching the sounds of the letters of the alphabet, and then emphasizes practice in blending them together to form words. After going over the alphabet, in lesson one, you will be using lessons two through sixty with your child. Most of the left-hand pages in these lessons consist of words that have a new sound; corresponding right-hand pages consist of sentences using these new words, which are just silly enough to make reading them a delight for your young child. By copying these sentences out below the examples, practice in writing will be gained as well.

Most of the words in this book will be familiar to your child. After all, the average five or six year old has a speaking vocabulary of over twenty thousand words. Learning to read one's native language, then, is not like learning a new language. It is, instead, the process of deciphering the written symbols that correspond to the spoken language that your child already knows very well. In fact, it is exactly like learning how to decipher a code, which is why phonics is often referred to as "decoding." Your children will find that "breaking the code" of the English language—that is, "sounding out" the letters and blending them into words—will be one of the most exciting "games" that they have ever played. It will be thrilling for the child to recognize words like "cat" or "mad" in the very first lessons. The excitement will only keep building as more and more words become recognizable, and are no longer merely abstract jumbles of letters. If you follow the plan in this book, and spend some time daily on each lesson, your child will soon be able to read just about anything that she sees in print! Because she already has an amazingly large vocabulary, she will certainly understand most of what she comes across in children's books, as well as simple adult books, newspapers, and magazines. If she runs into an unfamiliar word, she can easily ask an adult or older sibling its meaning, thereby increasing her vocabulary.

*But aren't there a lot of exceptions to the phonic "rules"?*

Once your child has learned all of the common letter sounds and combinations as presented in the sixty lessons, he will be able to read almost every word he sees with perfect pronunciation. The great majority of English words—estimates range from 87–94 %—do sound just the way they are spelled. About 10% of all words in the English language, and only 6% of the most commonly used words, are "exceptions" to the rules. For example, in the word "said" the "s" and the "d " have their normal sounds, yet the "ai" combination has an unexpected sound. Since these exception words are relatively few in number, however, they really do not present a problem. The most commonly used exception words are thoroughly covered in this book, and children generally delight in being told that there are a few words in which the vowels are "naughty" and don't follow the rules!

### What is the right age for a child to begin learning to read?

Over the past fifty years, a tremendous amount of research has been done on child development. A great deal of evidence points to the fact that there are certain "sensitive" periods in a child's life, when he or she is particularly able to learn specific skills. The Italian educator Dr. Maria Montessori concluded, and many studies have confirmed her findings, that the ideal age for a child to acquire reading skills is between the ages of four and six. From ages two to four children master the basics of spoken language; it is natural that mastering the written symbols for the same language that has just been learned at such an astonishing pace should immediately follow. The four-to-six year old child, then, has a unique capacity to learn to read, and will usually do so far more quickly and easily than a child who is either younger or older. There are, of course, some exceptions. Numerous cases of three year old children who have successfully learned to read have been documented. As well, some children are not ready to read until they are slightly older than six, for various reasons, including the natural variety in rates of human development. Yet the average child is ready to read at age four or five. (If your child is lucky enough to be able to attend a Montessori school, then he or she will learn, by the phonic method, to read at this age.)

Since your child is most receptive to attaining reading skills before he reaches first grade, it is a very good idea to teach him at home yourself. The first five years of your child's life are the most vitally important, in terms of his emotional, physical and intellectual growth. Many parents are unaware of the fact that a child's IQ is not something that is predetermined before birth. Rather, the level of intelligence that a child will achieve is directly related to the amount of intellectual stimulation he receives in his early years. By teaching your child to read at age four or five, you will be greatly expanding his intellectual capacity for the rest of his life. An excellent book that greatly expands on this theme is entitled *How to Raise a Brighter Child*, by Joan Beck, and is highly recommended reading.

A four or five year old who can read is rarely bored, and is likely to watch far less television than average. For, once he can read, he can occupy himself for hours on end, in a productive, stimulating, and challenging manner—exploring the infinite treasures that await him in the incredible world of books.

### Don't some "experts" oppose early reading?

There are those who oppose early reading on the grounds that it puts too much pressure on a child. Certainly, the child who is highly resistant to reading should not be pressured into doing so. The fact is, though, that most children at age four or five are extremely eager to learn new things, for learning is the greatest "game" that there is. The vast majority of children at this age are very interested in letters, words, books, reading and writing, and to deny them entry into the marvelous world of the printed page is surely wrong. Studies have not found a single case of any child who was damaged by having the ability to read at a young age! Many older children and adults, however, are profoundly grateful to their parents for having encouraged them to read early on.

### What should I do to help my child become ready to read?

One of the most important things that you can do for your child, from the time she is born, is to make sure that she is exposed to hearing the normal sounds of speech a great deal. Talk to your child as you are dressing her, feeding her, taking her for a walk, even if you know that she cannot understand what you are saying. Be sure that you sometimes speak to her in "adult" language, rather than just in "baby talk," for this is the best way to develop her ability to understand spoken language. Also, expose her to great music at home, and encourage her to play with simple musical instruments or musical toys, to further develop her auditory abilities.

One of the best ways to expose your child to spoken language, as well as to interest him in books, is to read aloud to him. Make this a regular part of your daily routine. Reading aloud should begin when your child is very young, as it will enhance his or her ability to later make the relationships between the sounds of letters and their printed form.

Another activity that will develop a child's keen interest in books is to have him dictate a story of his own to you. Write it down on large sheets of paper, and afterwards allow your child to illustrate it with his crayons. Staple the pages together, and he is the proud author of a new book! This activity works especially well with three and four year-olds.

Another important way to encourage your child's love of books is to give him his own bookshelf, and buy him as many books as you can. That does not mean that they have to be expensive ones. It is often very easy to obtain second-hand books in excellent condition at a yard sale, or used bookstore. Also, take him to the library often. Get him his own library card, and let him choose his own books from the hundreds of selections that even a small library usually has.

The very best thing that you can do, however, is to be a good model. Children love to imitate adults, especially their parents. Be sure that you keep lots of books, magazines, newspapers, etc., around the house, and spend some time reading in front of your child. He or she will learn, by your example, that reading is indeed one of life's most enjoyable and important experiences.

A very good book that gives further suggestions on developing your child's eagerness to learn to read is entitled *Give Your Child a Head Start in Reading*, by Fitzhugh Dodson, who has also written the bestselling books *How to Parent* and *How to Father*. This book also includes a comprehensive list of suggested books for reading aloud to your child, as well as a collection of Dodson's own wonderful modern rhymes that are sure to delight any child.

## Will my child be taught phonics in school?

For thousands of years, phonics has been used all over the world to teach reading in countries with alphabetic languages. Numerous studies have concluded that it remains the very best way for children to learn how to read in their native language. Phonics is still used to teach reading in France, Germany, Italy, Norway, Spain, the Soviet Union, etc. In these countries, almost all children are perfect readers by the time they are halfway through first grade. Remedial reading courses are practically non-existent, and cases of dyslexia are exceedingly rare.

Unfortunately, however, most public schools in the United States stopped teaching reading by the phonic method in the 1930's. Phonics was replaced with an experimental modern method called the sight method, which simply does not work very well. In fact, the U.S. now ranks only 49th worldwide in literacy rates; one third of adults have severe reading difficulties; and up to one third of all American children are classified as learning disabled or dyslexic. This national literacy crisis, which effects adults and children at all socio-economic levels, is in large measure caused by the ineffectiveness of the "sight" method as taught in our public schools.

## Just what is the sight method?

In the sight method, which is also known as the word method, or look-and-say method, children are not taught to associate letters with their corresponding sounds. Instead, they are taught to memorize whole words by the way they look. Sometimes pictures are shown along with words, as an aid to recognition. Of course, it is quite difficult to memorize whole words without having the ability to easily break them down into their component sounds. Therefore it is only possible to learn a few hundred words per year in this manner; and so the primers given to children in sight method reading programs have severely limited vocabularies. By the time they reach sixth grade, then, they are only able to read one or two thousand words—although their speaking vocabulary consists of tens of thousands of words. Because it is very difficult to memorize whole words in this way, it is necessary to repeat each word countless times, in order to help imprint it on the child's mind. Therefore, the reading material used in sight method programs has not only a severely limited vocabulary, but each word is endlessly repeated. Instead of being able to read about real and important events in a newspaper, or fascinating characters in the many wonderful children's stories that exist, sight method trained children are limited to reading very simplistic and dull material. This hardly provides them with an incentive to learn to read.

It would take a lifetime to memorize the thousands upon thousands of words in the English language one by one with the sight method; many children, therefore, simply give up in despair at some point, overwhelmed by the never-ending chore that reading appears to be.

## Then why do some children learn to read well in school?

While most American schools do not use phonic reading programs, some do. It is estimated that as of 1988 about 15–20 % of American public schools do use phonics for reading. Wherever phonics is used, whether it be an inner-city school or an upper-income suburban school, the results are always excellent, with very few students encountering reading difficulties.

As well, some schools are now using reading instruction methods that combine phonic elements with the sight method. If children are exposed to at least some of the letter/sound relationships they may be able to figure out the rest of the code for themselves. Although children taught by combination methods will not fare as well as those who are taught phonics in a comprehensive manner, they will at least have a somewhat better chance of becoming proficient readers.

The majority of American children, however, are taught by the sight method. Yet some of them do learn to read perfectly well. How does this happen? In every single case in which a child trained in the sight method reads well it is simply because he figured out the letter/sound relationships on his own. Perhaps he did this by occasionally asking a friend or parent questions about the sounds of the letters, made the connections when being read aloud to, or received clues from television commercials, where words are spoken and displayed on the screen at the same time.

Indeed, absolutely everyone who reads quickly and well reads by silently "sounding out" the words. That is what you are doing right at this moment. It happens instantaneously and unconsciously, but it happens nonetheless. The problem is, however, that sometimes even the brightest children do not come to realize the phonic principles on their own if they are never told about them at all; the wonderful potential of these children then becomes lost, as they slowly drift into the world of non-readers.

### Why don't the public schools just switch back to phonics?

If only it were that simple. Actually, even the U.S. Department of Education recommends that schools switch back to comprehensive phonics programs.

One part of the problem is that fashions prevail in education just as they do in clothing, music, food, architecture, etc. Much has been invested in the development of the sight method programs, in terms of teacher training, textbooks, etc. Many educational administrators are reluctant to make sweeping changes in their programs, even in the face of research that clearly shows that their current policies are counter-productive.

A highly recommended book which goes into far greater detail about this than can be covered here is the classic treatise on the subject, *Why Johnny Can't Read* by Rudolf Flesch. This book was first published in 1955, and along with its sequel, *Why Johnny Still Can't Read*, published in 1981, it describes the phonic/sight method debate at great length.

As an interested parent, however, you can try convincing your local elementary schools to reinstate phonics. There are some excellent phonics materials available for use in schools. Suggest that your school begin using a program such as that published by the Open Court Publishing Company, which is a particularly well-designed phonics program. Homeschooling parents have many excellent choices such as *Foundations* from Logic of English (LogicofEnglish.com), *Phonics Museum* from Veritas Press (veritaspress.com), or *Primary Arts of Language* from the Institute for Excellence in Writing (iew.com).

# About Handwriting

### *Just what is the style of handwriting taught in this book?*

The style taught here is called "Italic." It is the easiest style to learn, the fastest to write, extremely legible, and beautiful to look at.

While the style of printing that is usually taught to young children is certainly legible, it is extremely hard to do. One of the hardest tasks a child or an adult can perform is to make perfect circles. Yet in almost all the models of manuscript printing that are given to children, letters such as o, c, etc., are formed as perfect circles. These models are almost always mechanically made, rather than made by hand, for the very good reason that no adult can make them very well either! When children are given model letters that they cannot possibly duplicate, no matter how hard they try, they experience a vague sense of failure that discourages them from even wanting to practice writing.

The fact is, it is far more natural to make letters that are based on shapes that are closer to ovals than to circles. The simple form of Italic that is used throughout the sixty lessons in this book is a model that young children will actually have very little trouble imitating. This will foster a sense of self-confidence in them that will make them eager to practice writing, for it will be pleasurable rather than frustrating.

As you can see from the models shown here, the basic Italic letters are not radically different from the typical style of printing that children are taught. The differences are subtle, yet important. In addition to using oval rather than circular shapes, most of the Italic letters are made in one stroke, without lifting the pen, rather than several strokes as they are in typical printing. This too makes it far easier for your child to learn Italic.

### How does a simple Italic change into a fast style of handwriting?

Children under the age of seven are more comfortable writing in a somewhat larger size and at a fairly slow pace, and therefore the simple letter models used throughout the sixty lessons are suitable for them. To teach handwriting to an older child, however, it is advisable to first go over the alphabet, in Chapter Two, and then (if your child is not also using the reading lessons) proceed to Chapter Six.

This chapter provides step-by-step practice in making a transition from a basic upright Italic style, to a fast, semi-joined Italic suitable for everyday handwriting. The first stage of this transition is to begin writing the very same letter shapes, but with a slight slant to the right. (Left-handers may feel more comfortable continuing to write upright letters, however.) The next stage is to write these slanted letters in a smaller size; and then to learn certain joins that increase speed without hindering legibility. Finally, the option of writing with an edged or calligraphy pen is presented. It can take as little as a week or as much as several months to go through these stages, depending on the particular inclination of the student.

### Why do only some of the letters join together in fast Italic writing?

The fastest legible writing occurs when certain letters join each other, and others do not. The letters which naturally join each other are thoroughly presented in Chapter Six. Some letters, however, do not easily join into each other, and so to force them to do so actually takes extra time. Studies have shown that it is typically 25–50% slower to write an even, legible version of fully-joined script than it is to write an even, easy-to-read, only partially joined Italic.

Italic first developed in the Renaissance, as a faster way of writing the Humanist style of calligraphy (upon which our modern style of printing is based). For several hundred years, Italic was the prevailing style of handwriting used in Western Europe. Many variations of Italic existed, but for the most part, joins were employed as they are in this book, that is, they were used only when they occurred naturally.

Because fashions always have a way of changing, for better or for worse, by the eighteenth century Italic had evolved into a new style. In this new style, joins were used in all letter combinations, often achieved through the use of loops such as those in the letters *d g* etc. Until the early twentieth century, this new style, now called Copperplate, simply had to be written fairly slowly. The delicate nature of the pens then in use would not allow for very fast writing. Therefore, nineteenth century samples of this style often look fairly legible. Once the ballpoint pen, the fountain pen and our modern felt-tip pens came into use, however, it became possible to write this same looped, totally joined style very quickly. When written quickly, it usually degenerates greatly and becomes hard to read, as well as unattractive to look at.

1. Humanist was a style of writing used in the 1400's in Italy. Many printing types are still based on it.

2. When Humanist was written quickly, the letters became slanted and oval shaped. The Italic style, then, began as a fast version of Humanist.

3. By the late sixteenth century, Italic itself had evolved into a new style, called Copperplate.

4. Our modern script is based on Copperplate Because its extremely difficult to do Copperplate well, most Americans have ugly, illegible writing.

Even when written slowly and neatly, however, this style, which is still taught to the vast majority of American school children today, cannot compare in legibility to the Italic style. When letters are completely joined together, it is harder to distinguish one from another, and therefore it takes more time and effort to read them. This is why you have never seen a book, magazine or newspaper printed in a style resembling Copperplate!

This style, at its best, is used only as a decorative style, for wedding invitations or other special occasions in which legibility is not paramount.

## Will my child be taught Italic in school?

Unfortunately, just as most American schools use ineffective methods to teach reading, they also use ineffective methods of handwriting instruction. In fact, it was because students were having such tremendous difficulty learning to write script in the early twentieth century that educators decided to teach young children a simple unjoined style of printing first. Most schools today start children off with this style of printing, which is difficult enough in its own way, due to the circular forms of the letters. Then, after a year or two of this, children are made to switch gears altogether and learn the joined script style, which very rarely produces graceful legible writing, as attested to by the typical American scrawl.

What happens, then, is that children are taught the style that preceded Italic, historically, and then the style that it evolved into. Yet Italic itself is far easier to learn, faster to write, and more attractive than either one!

Italic is going through a revival world-wide, however. Schools in Sweden and Iceland now teach Italic to all schoolchildren. Select schools in England and the United States are beginning to realize the merits of Italic as well, and eventually it will become the standard style of handwriting nationwide.

## Why is handwriting important in this computer age?

First of all, most people do not have access to computers or even smart phones all the time. A student taking notes in a class or from reference works in a library often cannot use technology to do so. We all need to write checks, grocery lists, etc. almost daily. For practical reasons, then, it will always be necessary to do at least some of our writing by hand.

Having writing that is unattractive and difficult to read can be a source of great frustration, while having beautiful handwriting can be a source of deep satisfaction and pride. Handwriting is truly an art form and a wonderful means of self-expression. The basic Italic style presented here is a springboard, and everyone will ultimately develop their own unique variation of it. Studies in England have proven that children who write in Italic take a far greater interest in reading as well, and do better in all their school subjects. The greater self-confidence they gain from being able to achieve a beautiful and fluid handwriting spills over into all other aspects of life as well.

Beautiful handwriting should not be an exception; once Italic becomes standard in our schools, it can instead become the rule.

# Teaching Tips

## 1. Start with Chapter Two, by teaching your child the alphabet.

If he or she already knows how to print typical looking small letters, be sure that you point out the subtle ways in which the Italic letters are made differently. If your child does not already know the alphabet, it is a good idea to emphasize the sounds of the letters, rather than their names. Point out that the "a" shape has the sound that the word apple starts with, that the "b" shape sounds like "buh" as in ball, etc. It is critical that your child can identify the sounds of the letters, and can write each letter, even in a somewhat crude looking form, before you proceed on to lessons two through sixty. It is not likely that your four or five year old will have trouble learning the letter sounds. Yet if she is highly resistant to doing so, wait until she does express interest before trying again.

## 2. Be very encouraging and patient as your child proceeds.

Emphasize to your child that the idea is to recognize each letter or letter combination, say its sound, and blend the sounds together to make a word. At first, your child may experience some difficulty in blending, or "sounding out" the words. Encourage him by praising him greatly when he says a word correctly. When he makes a mistake, gently ask him to try again.

Each lesson consists of a list of words with the new sound, and some words are repeated. By going over each page several times, your child should grasp the new sound. Some lessons are easier than others. If your child becomes discouraged because a particular sound is giving him trouble, be especially careful to be very encouraging. Never let him feel hurried or criticized. If he simply isn't in the mood for learning on a given day, skip it and postpone the lesson until he is ready to try again.

If your child is unfamiliar with a certain word and asks you the meaning, stop and take the time to explain it to him. You may even wish to show him how words can be looked up in a dictionary for children.

The sentences on the writing practice pages are deliberately meant to be silly, so that your child will find that learning to read is really more like a fun game than a chore to be gotten through.

### 3. Make the lesson part of your daily or evening routine.

Try to spend some time every day, if possible, going over the reading lessons with your child, and let him spend as much time as he wishes with his writing practice. Begin by reviewing the previous day's reading lesson, and possibly skimming over the last few lessons that you have covered, asking your child to read a few words here and there to refresh his memory about specific letter sounds.

It is quite possible that your child could complete the lessons within sixty days. However, children do learn at different rates. Some children may need to spend at least a few days on each lesson before going on to the next. Do not be concerned if your child seems to forget what he learned the day before, and needs to repeat the lessons several times. There really is no reason to hurry. Whether your child takes sixty days or six months is really not important. W hat is important is that learning to read should be an immensely enjoyable and enriching experience for your child every step of the way, regardless of the time frame involved. Never pressure him to go faster than he wishes. He will let you know what pace is comfortable for him.

### 4. Do not expect your four or five year olds' writing to look as even or neat as the model letters.

The word lists in the reading lessons are written out by hand specifically so that your child will have good models of real handwriting to imitate. He may trace over these word lists for additional practice if he wishes. O n the right hand pages, he will be copying out the silly sentences, which will be excellent writing practice. It will take time for him to acquire a truly consistent, even look to his writing. By age six or seven, his motor coordination will improve and then his writing will take on a higher quality.

Do make some photocopies of the blank guidesheet at the end of the alphabet chapter (page 38), and allow your child to use these for additional writing practice. Encourage him to be creative and to make up silly sentences or stories of his own. At first, he may spell words incorrectly, using consonant sounds appropriately, and vowel sounds inappropriately. The important thing is that he is making the connection between letters and their sounds; this is actually a fine way to develop early phonic abilities, so allow him to write in this manner if he wishes. Later on, you can gently remind him of the correct usage of the vowels in his writing.

It will be obvious whether your child is left or right-handed, by the hand he chooses to use most of the time. About ten percent of children are naturally left-handed, and should not be forced to switch to their right hands.

### 5. Continue reading aloud to your child.

Reading aloud to your child while she is going through the process of learning to read will be especially valuable. She will be thrilled to find that she can now read at least some of the words on the page that you are reading to her! Reading aloud reinforces the relationship between the letters and sounds as nothing else can. Even when your child can read totally on her own, however, reading aloud is an activity that should be continued. In this way, parent and child together can continue to share the special wonder and magic of the world of books.

### If your child has difficulty

Please note that if your child has great difficulty proceeding through the lessons in this hook, you should simply wait and try teaching him again later. If you are still not successful, it may he that your child actually does have special learning needs. Most cases of learning disorders are misdiagnosed, and are a result of poor teaching methods; yet a small percentage of children do have special needs which are best met by a competent, caring professional.

Most likely, however, you will be amazed and delighted with your child's new found skills in reading and writing within a few months time of using this book.

You will be setting your child on the joyous road of learning for the rest of his or her life. May it be a wonderful journey!

**Notes**

# Chapter 2.

## The Alphabet

## The Alphabet

In this section the vowels are presented first so that you can emphasize that these letters are different from the consonants. Tell your child that most of the time the vowels will sound the way they do in the words associated with the pictures shown here. The letter "a" will sound as it does in "apple", the letter "e" will sound as it does in "elephant", etc. Make sure your child understands that vowels will sometimes change and have different sounds, unlike consonants which *almost* always sound the same. The letter "c," of course, is an exception. Teach your child that the letter "c" will usually have the "hard" sound of "cup" throughout the beginning lessons.

Have your child trace over the letters using a pencil. Then he or she can practice them on notebook paper, or the photocopies that you may wish to make of the ruled sheet at the end of this chapter.

It is generally best to keep the paper (or book) straight, rather than slanted, while writing. Left-handers, however, may wish to slant their paper to the left to make writing more comfortable.

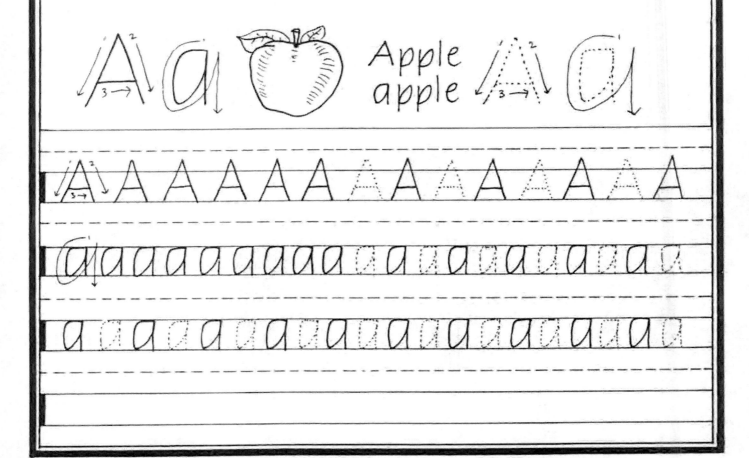

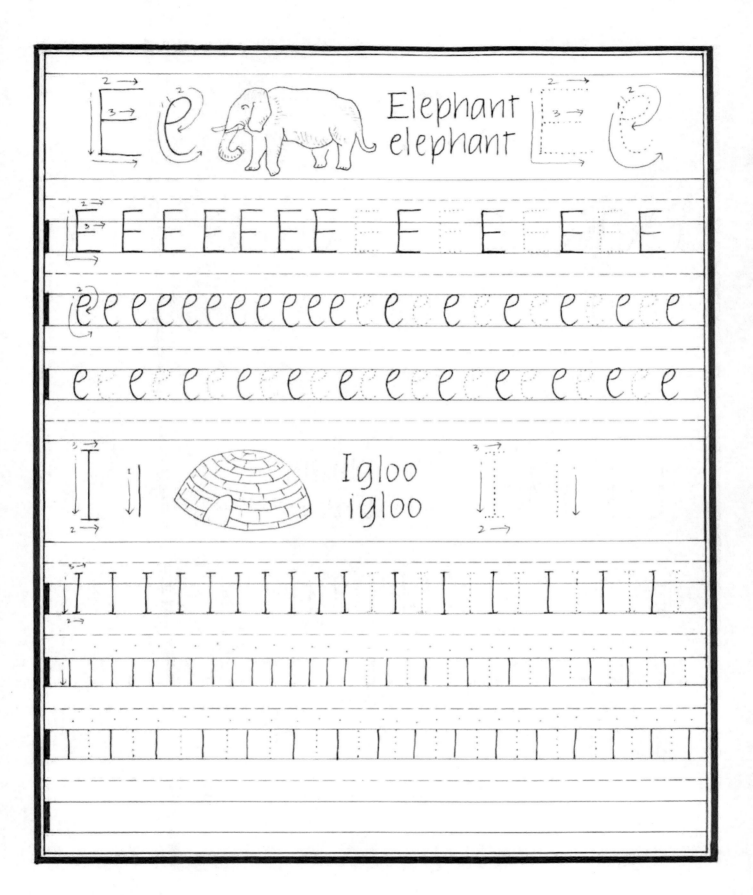

Elephant
elephant

Igloo
igloo

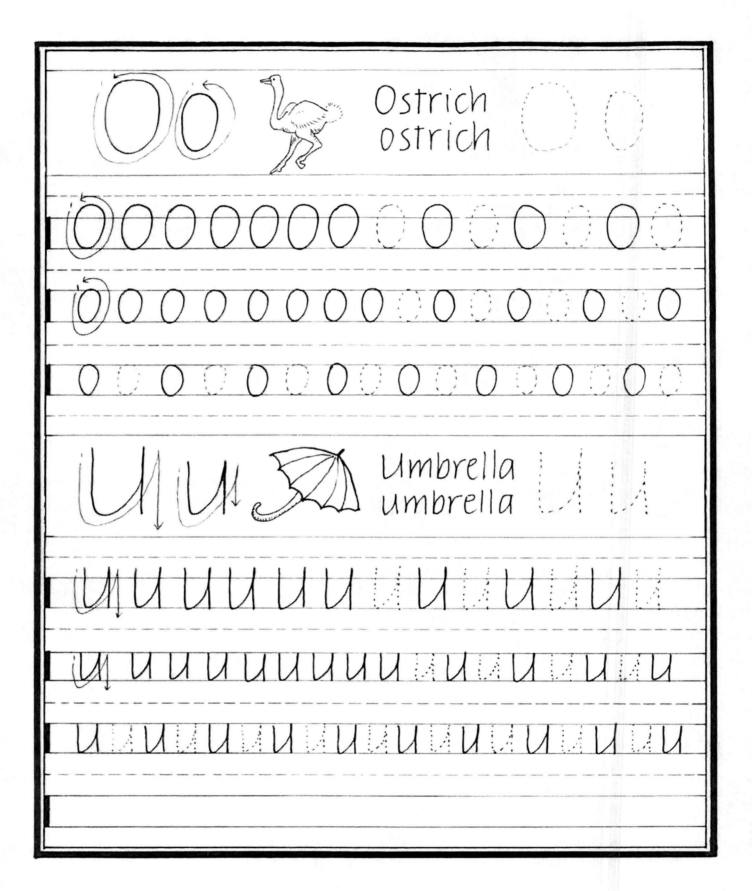

Ostrich
ostrich

Umbrella
umbrella

# Consonants

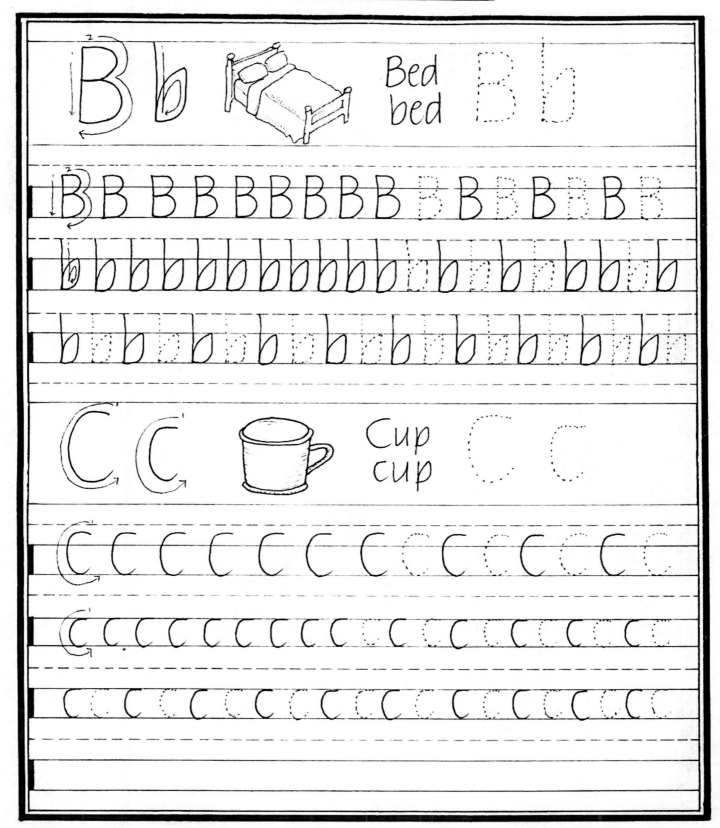

Bed
bed

Cup
cup

D d Door door D d

D D D D D D D D D D D D D

Be sure to make d in two parts: make this shape first: O O O O O O d Then add the long straight part d d d

d d d d d d d d d d d d d

F f Fish fish F f

F F F F F F F F F F F F F

f f f f f f f f f f f f f f f

f f f f f f f f f f f f

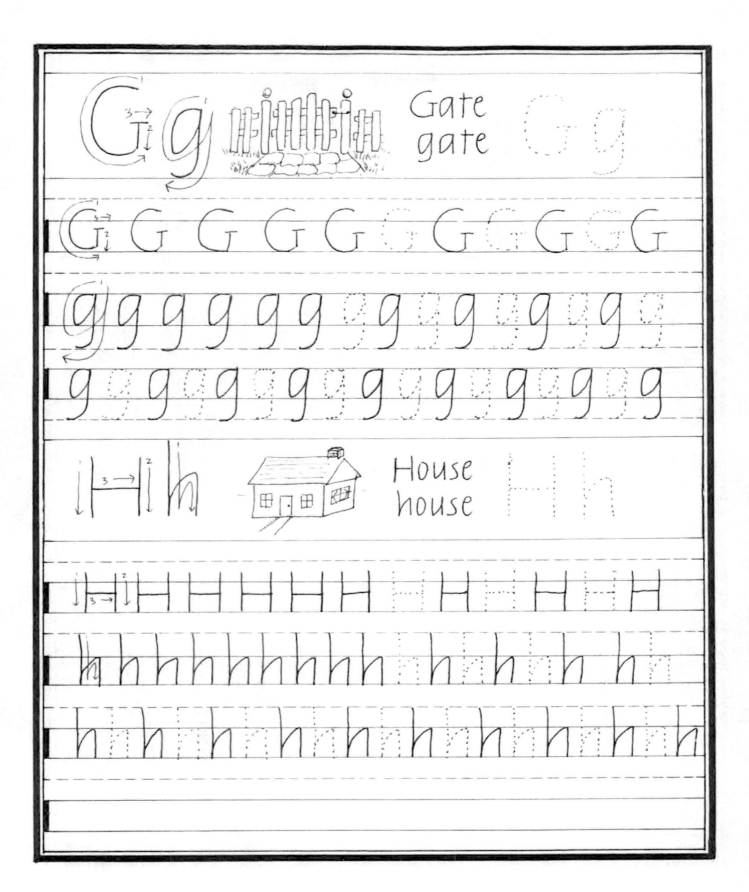

Gate
gate

House
house

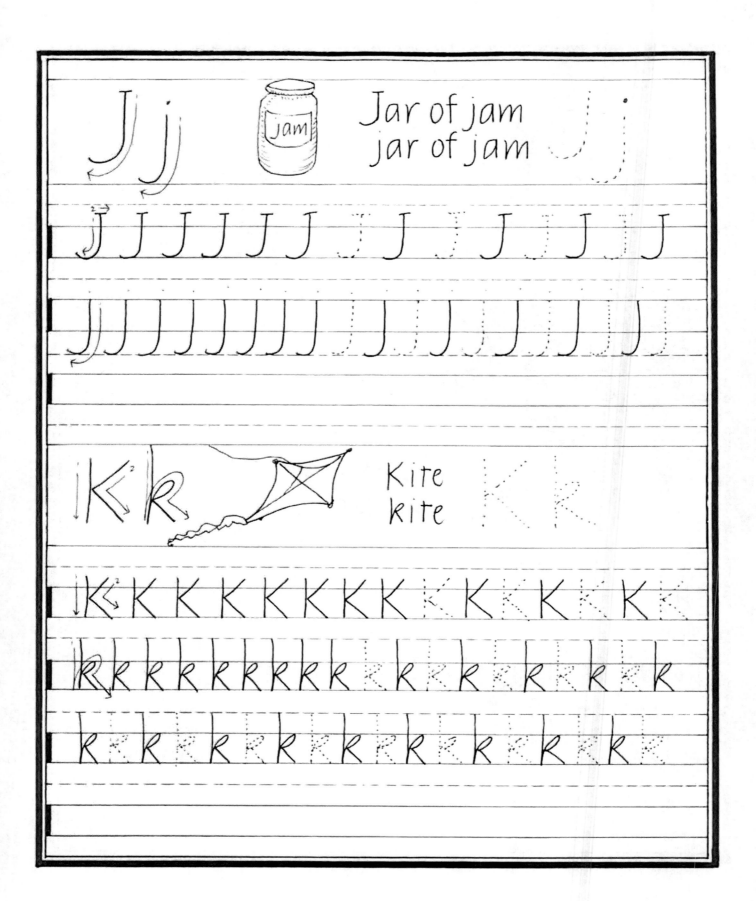

J j    Jar of jam
       jar of jam

Kite
kite

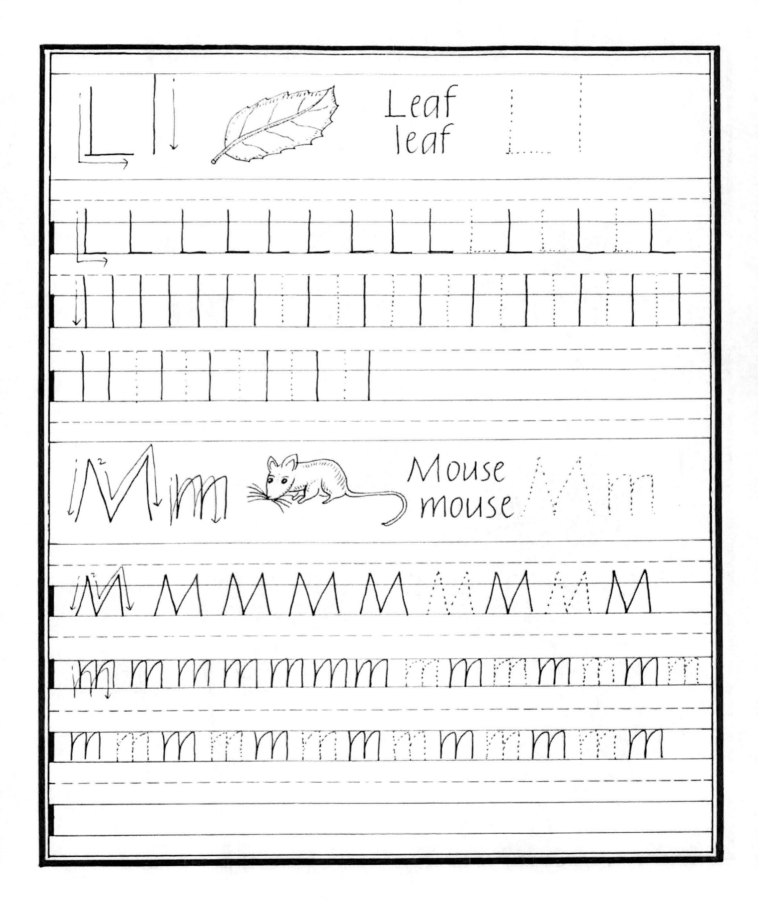

Leaf
leaf

Mouse
mouse

Nn    Nose
        nose    Nn

Pp    Pear
        pear    Pp

p is made in
two strokes:

be sure to start the
second stroke right here →

Qu qu   Queen   Qu
queen

A q is <u>always</u> followed by u.

Qu Qu Qu

qu qu qu qu qu qu qu qu qu qu

qu qu qu qu qu qu qu qu qu qu

Rr   Rose   Rr
rose

R R R R R R R R R R

r r r r r r r r r r r r r

r r r r r r r r r r r r r

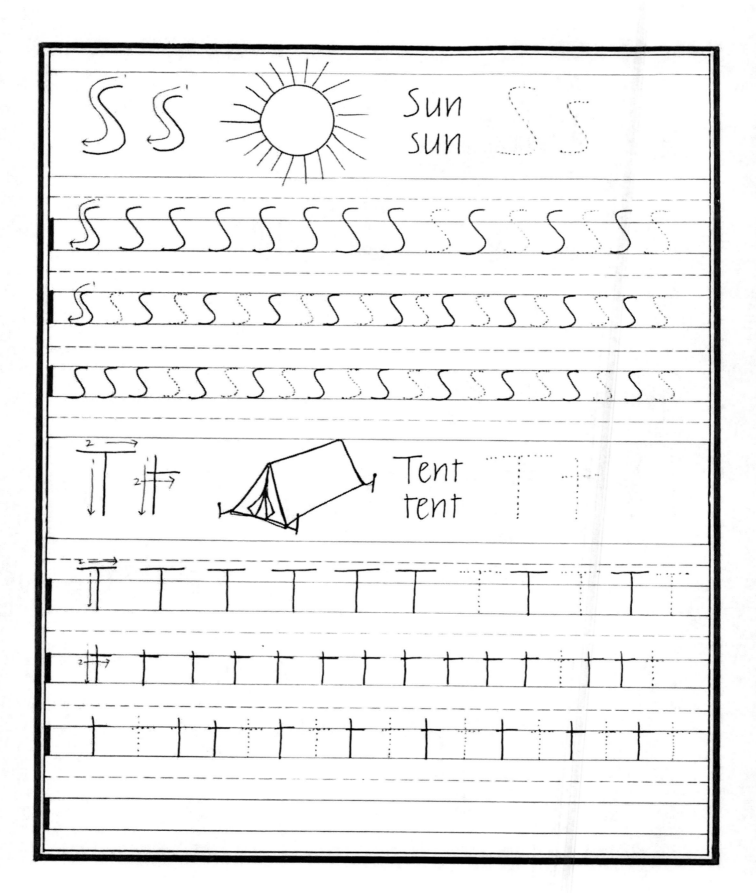

Sun
sun

Tent
tent

Violin
violin

Window
window

41

Xylophone
xylophone

Yawn
yawn

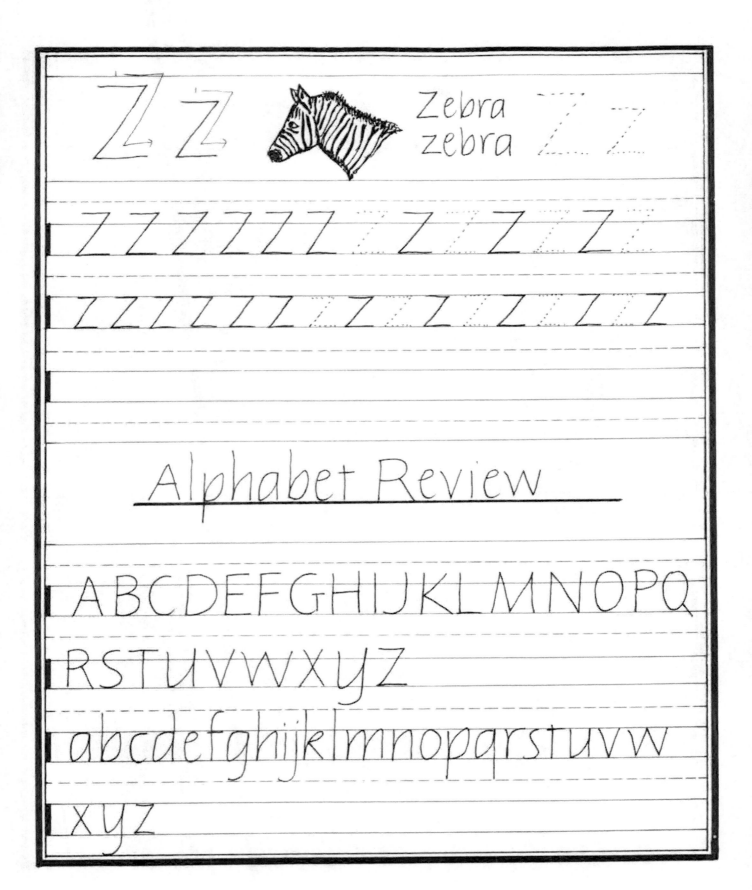

Z z        Zebra
           zebra        Z z

Z Z Z Z Z Z Z Z Z Z Z Z

Z Z Z Z Z Z Z Z Z Z Z Z

Alphabet Review

ABCDEFGHIJKLMNOPQ
RSTUVWXYZ
abcdefghijklmnopqrstuvw
xyz

43

# Chapter 3.

## Lessons 2 - 23

Short Vowel Sounds
Consonant Blends
Plural Words
Compound Words
Words with "or" Sound
Short Words that end in Vowels

# Lesson 2 - Short a

| | | | | | |
|---|---|---|---|---|---|
| at | bag | am | mad | nap | quack |
| bat | tag | Ann | Dad | map | rack |
| hat | lag | van | Dan | cap | sack |
| cat | sag | tan | ham | rap | cat |
| sat | gag | man | am | tap | mat |
| mat | wag | can | jam | lap | as |
| far | nag | fan | Sam | gap | has |
| rat | as | ran | yam | sap | have |
| pat | gas | pan | dab | back | had |
| ax | mass | can | gab | hack | mad |
| tax | pass | add | lab | jack | hat |
| Max | jazz | had | tab | lack | sat |
| wax | has | has | bat | tack | fat |
| pat | pal | bad | at | has | am |
| cat | gal | sad | | | |
| mat | at | pad | | | |

have sounds like hav

46

Pat a fat cat, Max! Can a

Pat

bat have a hat? Dad had

bat

ham, Ann had jam. A bad

ham,

mad rat sat on a bat. A sad

mad

fat cat sat on a cap. Dan has

has

a yam, Sam has a sack.

# Lesson 3 - Short e

| | | | | | |
|---|---|---|---|---|---|
| met | yes | red | pet | set | tell |
| wet | less | fed | peg | sell | ten |
| jet | mess | led | men | net | web |
| pet | web | wed | met | vet | yet |
| yet | hem | bell | yet | leg | get |
| get | pep | tell | yell | let | bet |
| set | egg | yell | ten | sell | bell |
| let | leg | sell | tell | set | keg |
| vet | peg | fell | wet | deck | leg |
| net | beg | well | hem | neck | sell |
| bet | keg | get | fell | net | let |
| men | Meg | mess | egg | jet | deck |
| pen | deck | bell | let | met | bed |
| ten | peck | | | | |
| den | Ed | | | | |
| yen | bed | | | | |

Other words with short e sound:

said, says, been, again

yes, ten men had a wet red hen.

A bad cat fell in a well.

Max met a mad bat, Dan

fed a sad cat. Ann let an egg

get wet. Sam said, "A pet fell

in a net."

# Lesson 4-Short i

| | | | | | |
|---|---|---|---|---|---|
| it | hid | if | hill | lick | bit |
| bit | it | is | quill | pick | fit |
| hit | tip | his | till | sick | dip |
| sit | nip | fizz | pill | tick | jig |
| fit | rip | quiz | fill | quick | miss |
| kit | sip | wiz | mill | kick | pig |
| wit | lip | hiss | in | it | sit |
| quit | zip | miss | win | zip | fib |
| pit | dip | kiss | bin | wig | hit |
| fib | wig | him | fin | hit | rip |
| bib | pig | dim | kin | rim | it |
| rib | jig | rim | tin | pill | is |
| lid | rig | ill | pin | mix | his |
| bid | big | bill | din | his | bib |
| kid | fix | sill | sin | is | kid |
| did | mix | kill | in | if | did |

A big fat pig did a jig. A

bad kid hid his bib. Kiss a

cat, miss a fat rat! A sick

pig had a big wet wig! A cat

bit a mad rat, a rat sat on a

wet hat.

# Lesson 5 - Short o

| | | | | | |
|---|---|---|---|---|---|
| Bob | dot | on | lock | mop | job |
| job | not | Mom | dock | top | sob |
| gob | nod | Tom | mock | hop | sod |
| sob | pod | on | rock | gone | cot |
| rob | rod | ox | sock | box | dot |
| mob | sod | box | jot | Bob | not |
| cob | odd | fox | lot | pop | pot |
| cot | cod | lox | lock | fox | gone |
| not | cop | pox | cob | top | on |
| hot | hop | jog | cod | Mom | tot |
| pot | top | fog | cot | hog | mob |
| tot | mop | log | cop | hop | odd |
| lot | pop | hog | hot | pox | got |
| rot | rob | mop | rot | hot | box |
| got | mob | | | | |
| jot | oz | | | | |

Sound-alike word: gone

52

yell at a pig, have a big fig.

Yell

Pet a fox, kiss an ox. Fill a

Pet

cup, sit on a bug. Get a net,

cup,

pet a red hen. Bob fed his

pet

fox to a big bad ox. "Sit a bit,"

fox

said a cat to a rat.

# Lesson 8 - Writing Review

Trace and copy the letters below.

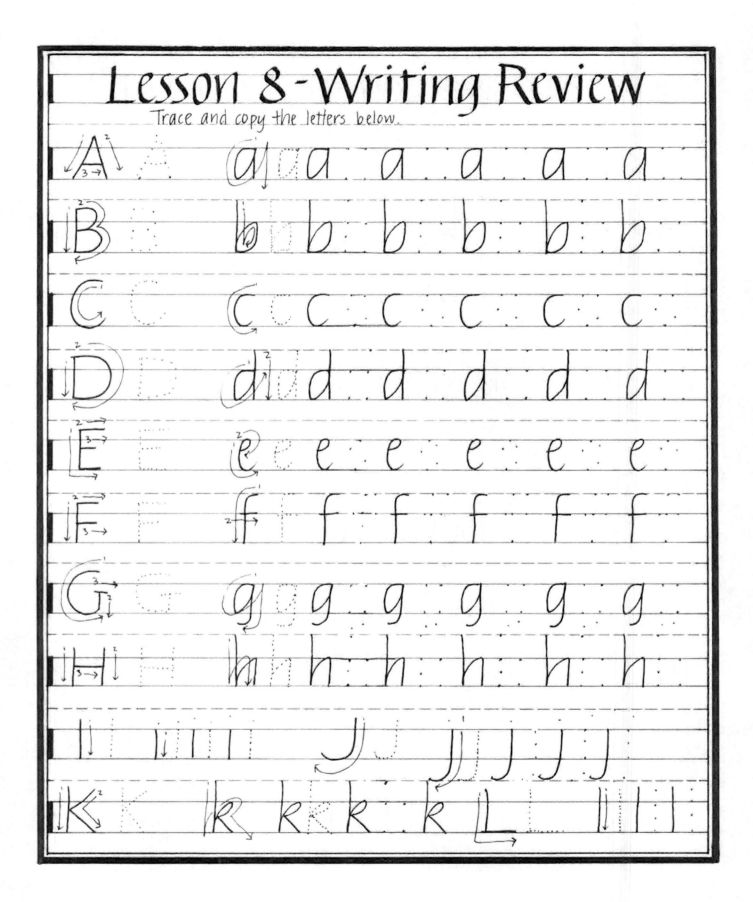

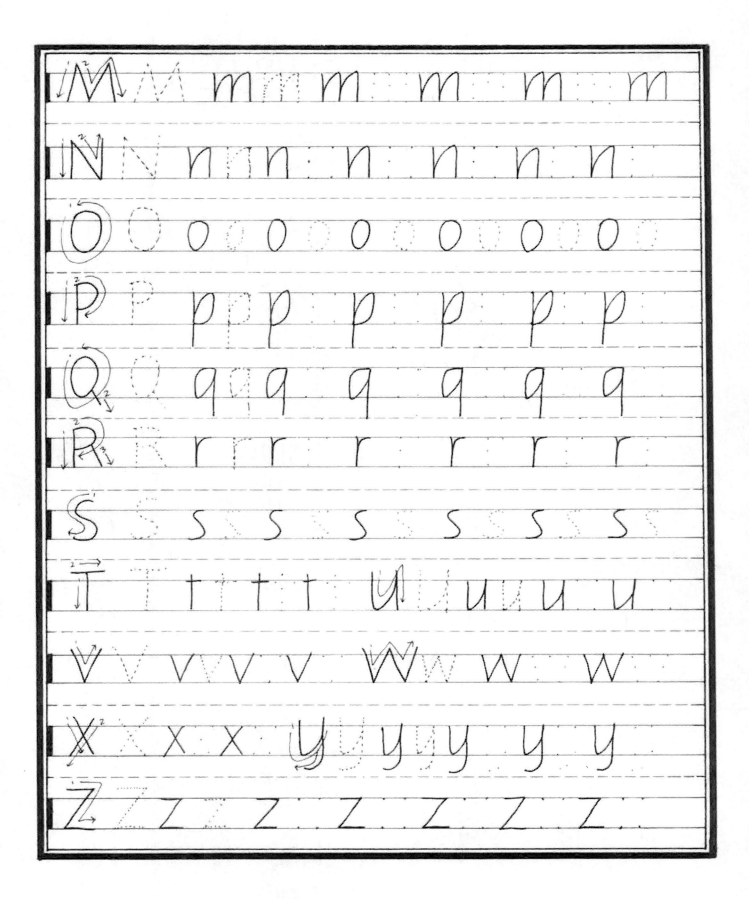

# Lesson 9 - Blending with s

**sm**
smell
smog
smack

**sn**
snug
sniff
snack
snuck
snap
snip

**squ**
squat
squid
squad

**sp**
spell
spit
spat
spin
spill

**sw**
swell
swim
swam
swap
swan

**spl**
split
splat

**sl**
slip
slap
slit
slot
slat
slop
slam
slack

**sc**
scar
scat

**spr**
sprig

**sk**
skit
skill
skin
skip

**st**
stick
stop
step
stab
staff
stack
stud
stun

Sit in a crib, crack a rib.

Sit

Drop an egg, trap a pig.

Drop

Trip on a step, tap on a

Trip

drum. Cross a log, trick a

drum

frog. Grab a hat, and a bat.

frog

# Lesson 11 - Blending with l

| bl | gl | cl | pl |
|---|---|---|---|
| block | glad | clap | plan |
| bless | glass | clock | plod |
| blob | gloss | clip | plum |
| blot | | class | plug |

**sl**
slip

**fl**

| fl | sl | cl | pl |
|---|---|---|---|
| flap | slip | clasp | plan |
| flop | slam | clam | plod |
| flip | slop | clad | plum |
| flag | slab | | |
| flick | slack | | |
| flat | slap | | |
| flask | slat | | |
| fled | slick | | |
| flex | slob | | |
| fluff | slug | | |
| | slum | | |

## lf, lb, lt, lk

| | | |
|---|---|---|
| elf | melt | bulk |
| self | belt | elf |
| bulb | felt | help |
| help | milk | gulp |
| gulp | silk | belt |
| pulp | sulk | bulb |

Help! A big black blob is

Help

on a block! His cat is flat,

on

his sled is red." Have a gulp

his

of milk," said an elf to himself.

of

"A plum was on a drum," said

A

a bug to a slick slug.

# Lesson 12 - Blending with n

| nd | nt | ng | nk |
|---|---|---|---|
| and | bent | sing | tank |
| band | ant | king | sank |
| land | pant | bring | prank |
| sand | went | brunt | stank |
| brand | tent | fang | plank |
| bend | sent | pang | clank |
| send | hint | sang | blank |
| mend | flint | spring | bank |
| lend | mint | sprang | blink |
| end | tint | wing | ink |
| fond | dent | gang | link |
| pond | lent | rung | junk |
| bond | rant | ring | dunk |
| strand | print | rang | sunk |
| stand | runt | bang | stink |

Dunk a skunk, bring a king.

Dunk

A big tank sank as a fat cat

A

drank. Does a bat have a

drank

wing, can a bug sting? Mend

wing

a tent, it is bent. Stand on a

a

plank, sing to a king.

# Lesson 13 - mp, tw, dw, xt, pt, ct, ft

| mp | tw, dw | pt | ct |
|---|---|---|---|
| lamp | twin | apt | act |
| lump | dwell | rapt | tact |
| damp | twig | opt | pact |
| dump | twist | kept | fact |
| bump | dwarf | | |
| jump | | | |
| pump | **xt** | | |
| hump | next | | |
| plump | text | | |
| stump | | | |
| mumps | | | |
| clump | | | |
| lump | | | |
| pump | | | |

## Silly Sentences

Jump on a log, hop on a frog. Ted kept his plump duck in a damp sack. It is a fact his duck had a twin.

A plump cat sat on a stump,

A

a bad cat jumps on a hat.

a

Does a sad slug dwell in a pit?

D

A brass lamp sat in some

A

grass, a big pig drank from

glass

a glass.

# Lesson 14 - ch, tch blends

## ch

| | |
|---|---|
| chum | check |
| pinch | chop |
| much | chap |
| such | chest |
| lunch | chick |
| hunch | chill |
| punch | pinch |
| munch | branch |
| chunk | brunch |
| chin | rich |
| chip | such |
| quench | chip |
| trench | punch |
| bench | much |
| clinch | bunch |

## tch

| | |
|---|---|
| latch | switch |
| batch | pitch |
| catch | ditch |
| match | hitch |
| snatch | fetch |
| scratch | itch |
| hatch | snatch |
| crutch | match |
| switch | fetch |
| ditch | catch |
| hitch | stitch |
| fetch | switch |
| stitch | crutch |
| itch | catch |
| notch | snatch |

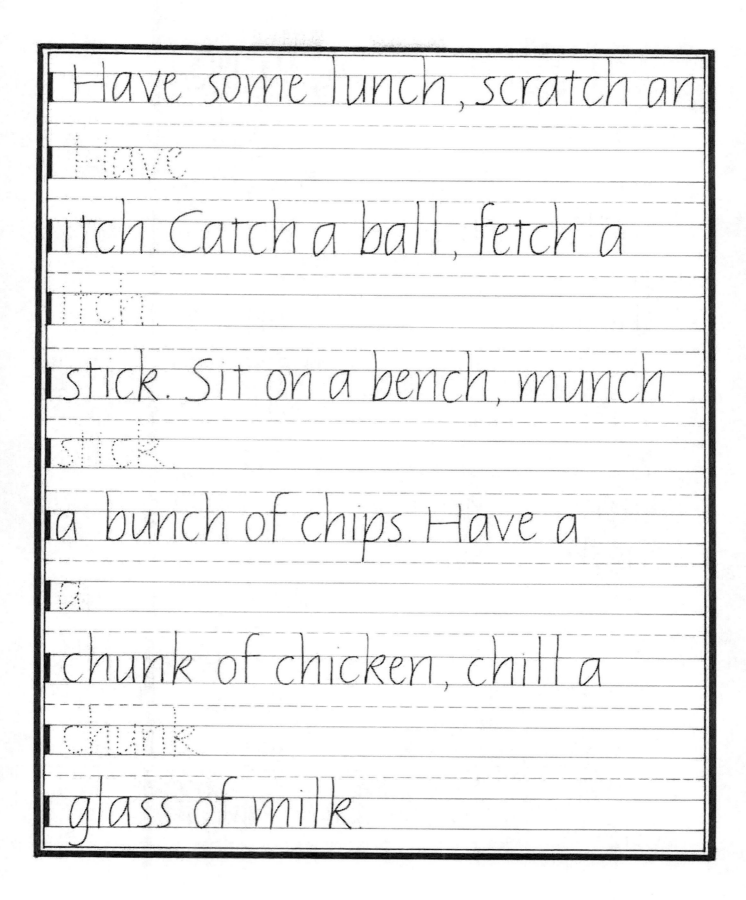

Have some lunch, scratch an

Have.

itch. Catch a ball, fetch a

itch.

stick. Sit on a bench, munch

stick

a bunch of chips. Have a

a

chunk of chicken, chill a

chunk

glass of milk.

# Lesson 15 - sh, th blends

| sh | | th (hard sound) | th (soft sound) |
|---|---|---|---|
| ship | dash | the | thin |
| shall | rush | this | think |
| shed | gush | then | thing |
| shell | mush | than | thick |
| shut | wish | them | thump |
| shift | fish | that | thank |
| dash | selfish | with | thrash |
| rash | shred | within | thrush |
| mash | shrill | the | thug |
| ash | dash | than | thicket |
| lash | ship | this | smith |
| crash | shot | them | thank |
| bash | shred | that | thin |
| sash | | | |
| cash | | | |

Sound-alike words: sure sounds like shor
sugar sounds like shugar

72

Which dwarf has a twin,

Which

which fish has a fin?

which

When will the bad witch

when

melt the king? What is that

melt

big black frog singing?

big

75

# Lesson 17 - Adding s or es

Add s to most words to make them mean more than one of something.
(a cat, six cats)

| | | |
|---|---|---|
| pig, pigs | pot, pots | mat, mats |
| egg, eggs | bug, bugs | bed, beds |
| cap, caps | tack, tacks | web, webs |
| flag, flags | rack, racks | rib, ribs |
| blob, blobs | cat, cats | kid, kids |
| plum, plums | hat, hats | sock, socks |
| pen, pens | peg, pegs | block, blocks |
| hand, hands | leg, legs | lock, locks |
| tent, tents | jug, jugs | gun, guns |
| cup, cups | rug, rugs | scar, scars |
| nest, nests | pest, pests | fist, fists |
| clam, clams | plug, plugs | belt, belts |
| ant, ants | band, bands | fang, fangs |
| twig, twigs | fact, facts | chip, chips |

Some words need an _es_ instead of just an s at the end.

axes  buses  fusses  presses  dresses
riches  lunches  scratches  switches

Some words have an s at the end to show that someone else is doing something. If you are talking _about_ yourself or _to_ someone else you would say:

<u>Pick</u> up a sock, <u>grab</u> a cap.

But if you are talking _about_ someone else, you would say:

Tim <u>picks</u> up his socks, and <u>grabs</u> his cap.

| | | | |
|---|---|---|---|
| rests | pops | skips | gulps |
| adds | comes | stops | claps |
| splits | huffs | swims | clasps |
| sells | puffs | spills | twists |
| sets | runs | slaps | jumps |
| fibs | rubs | slops | chops |
| rips | smells | slips | shreds |

# Lesson 18-Compound Words

exit
hamster
bathtub
robins
napkin
lobster
chicken
locket
rocket
pockets
kitchen
goblins
basket
quicksand
stocking
lipstick

frosting
mixup
ketchup
zigzag
biggest
within
dishpan
tomcat
lemons
pumpkin
visits
until
began
children
demand
garden

happens
important
husband
itself
president
result
something
under
admit
cannot
common
finish
forest
market
sudden
become

A rabbit will kiss a big pig

A

and a fat lobster in a basket.

and

A goblin with some red

A

slippers is in the bathtub!

slippers

A bad tomcat snuck into the

A

biggest rocket with a fish!

# Lesson 19 - Magic e

When the letter e comes at the end of a word, most of the time it has the magic effect of making the first vowel say it's name Carefully read the word pairs below. The e is silent, remember.

| | | |
|---|---|---|
| hid - hide | cod - code | gap - gape |
| din - dine | can - cane | van - vane |
| dim - dime | mat - mate | fin - fine |
| pan - pane | hat - hate | rip - ripe |
| pin - pine | fad - fade | kit - kite |
| tub - tube | rod - rode | rob - robe |
| car - care | cub - cube | not - note |
| man - mane | pal - pale | rod - rode |
| at - ate | star - stare | cut - cute |
| pet - pete | fat - fate | tap - tape |
| rid - ride | bit - bite | spit - spite |
| bon - bone | mad - made | slat - slate |
| rat - rate | bar - bare | scar - scare |
| sam - same | cap - cape | grip - gripe |

Hide that bone in the closet,

Hide

quick! Pete ate ten cubes

quick

of sugar, and it made him

of

sick. Ann likes fine red kites,

sick

but hates cats that bite!

but

# Lesson 20 - More Magic e

| | | | |
|---|---|---|---|
| late | bake | shake | hole |
| mane | cake | wade | cole |
| smile | rake | made | pole |
| pile | snake | shade | mole |
| hole | make | grade | stole |
| mole | take | parade | make |
| stole | brake | trade | cake |
| slope | slide | here | hide |
| hope | hide | mere | pile |
| cope | glide | frame | stride |
| rope | ride | lame | tide |
| mope | wife | same | side |
| dive | strife | sale | confide |
| hive | fife | stale | alive |
| alive | sake | pale | dive |
| pride | lake | male | rake |

Bake a cake, ride a snake.

Bake

Watch a parade, drink some

Watch

lemonade. Smile at a fish,

lemonade

make a wish. A mole stole

make

a pole, and hid it in a hole.

a

# Lesson 21 - Magic e Exceptions

Sometimes the magic doesn't work — some words keep their first vowel <u>short</u>, and the e at the end is still silent.

<u>give</u> sounds like giv   <u>have</u> sounds like hav

<u>live</u> sometimes sounds like liv (and sometimes it sounds like live with a long i)

<u>were</u> sounds like wer   <u>are</u> sounds like ar

give live give have were are give
live give have were are give live

---

These words have a short u sound, with a silent e at the end.

<u>come</u> sounds like cum   <u>some</u> sounds like sum

<u>one</u> sounds like wun   <u>above</u> sounds like abuv

come some one someone come
one come some some come one

---

Sometimes <u>ere</u> rhymes with "care"

<u>there</u> sounds like thare   <u>where</u> sounds like ware

there where there where there

Does Dad have one plum?

Does

Ann has some baskets of

Ann

rabbits to give Sam. Does

rabbits

that snake live in there above

that

the plump chipmunk? Come

the

on, where is that bad cat?

# Lesson 22 - or sound

| or | storm | torch | thorn | doctor | or |
|----|-------|-------|-------|--------|-----|
| for | torn | porch | lord | actor | for |
| corn | sort | fort | short | corn | your |
| cord | born | horn | shorn | torn | or |
| sport | form | snort | normal | | |
| port | pork | stork | north | | |
| worn | cork | scorn | adorn | | |

Sound-alike word

your <sup>sounds like</sup> yor

*Sound-alike word*
*your sounds like yor*

These words have the exact same "or" sound as the words above. They are exceptions to the "magic e" words, just like come, are and one.

| bore | sore | shore | pore | bore | explore |
|------|------|-------|------|------|---------|
| ore | lore | adore | store | core | restore |
| core | gore | before | core | more | chore |
| more | fore | more | snore | tore | adore |
| tore | chore | tore | bore | lore | before |
| store | snore | explore | sore | pore | store |
| pore | score | restore | lore | gore | snore |

Have some more corn, the

Have

doctor said. Before the big,

doctor

wet storm a torch was lit

wet

on the porch. It is normal to

on

be short when you are born.

be

# Lesson 23 - Short Words Ending in Vowels

Usually when there's only one vowel in a word and it's on the end, it says its name.

| | | | | | |
|---|---|---|---|---|---|
| be | he | we | she | hi | no |
| go | so | I | also | hello | no |
| we | be | she | so | go | he |

(Sometimes y sounds like a long i, and this is true in the words my )
and by .

---

Sometimes words with only one vowel at the end have a sound different than their own vowel. In all the words below, the o sounds like u instead, and in "two" and "who" the w is silent.

to    sounds like   tu

two   sounds like   tu   (the w is silent )

do    sounds like   du

who   sounds like   hu   ( the w is silent)

One very important word has a silent o in the middle.

you   sounds like   yu

Who are you ? Do not go to the store. Two goblins went to the bank.

88

Are you a big bug on a bike?

I did not think so! We will

go to the fort to say hello to

the two short storks who live

there. He said that he ate a

thorn for lunch!

You can ride upon a snake,

you

if you give me a big fat cake.

if

I will go to the store with you,

I

if you drink a fish for me.

if

We will ride to the lake, and

We

hide from the snake.

# Chapter 4.

## Lessons 24-41

## Vowel Combinations & Special Sounds

# Lesson 24 - Long a Combinations

Remember how a magic e makes a first vowel say its name? Sometimes when two vowels are right next to each other the second one works like a magic e. The second vowel has to be quiet and let the first vowel say its name. Sometimes the letter y is a vowel, and on this page it acts like one. All these ai and ay words have a <u>long</u> a sound like in the word care.

| <u>ai</u> | aid | fair | <u>ay</u> | slay | day |
|------|-------|--------|--------|---------|------|
| pail | raid | raisin | bay | stay | clay |
| pair | laid | saint | day | stray | lay |
| pain | maid | bait | say | ray | say |
| paint | tail | drain | hay | lay | today |
| fail | sail | ail | may | gay | may |
| faint | brain | paid | play | way | day |
| main | grain | stairs | clay | display | gray |
| train | chain | plain | pray | dismay | hay |
| rain | chair | hair | tray | subway | say |
| aim | faith | strain | relay | | |
| waist | mail | pair | today | | |
| braid | snail | main | fray | | |

Important Exception: Remember that <u>said</u> sounds like <u>sed</u>

Do you like to play with gray

Do

trains in the rain? Paint a

trains

pair of snails, stay and play

pair

with clay today. Bring me a

with

pail of snails and raisins. Do

Do

you have a tail, maybe?

# Lesson 25-aw Sound

In all these words, the letter a has the same sound it makes in awful.

| aw | | au | | |
|---|---|---|---|---|
| awful | raw | auto | cause | fault |
| law | claw | paul | because | maul |
| jaw | | haul | clause | haul |
| paw | **ar** | haunt | flaunt | auto |
| hawk | war | august | taunt | august |
| claw | wart | | | |
| draw | warm | **al, all, alt, ald, alk** (the l is silent in lk) | | |
| slaw | swarm | all | ball | squall |
| straw | ward | also | stall | call |
| lawn | water | call | wall | hall |
| flaw | war | tall | bald | halt |
| jigsaw | warm | hall | scald | chalk |
| saw | water | mall | malt | balk |
| squaw | warm | fall | salt | talk |
| | | small | wall | recall |

Sound-alike word: dog (sounds like dawg)

94

Raw snails taste awful ! Just

Raw

because it is a warm August

because

day, a tall hawk cannot play

day

ball on the lawn ! I saw him

ball

fall in the water backwards.

fall

All the small men ate eggs.

# Lesson 26 - ar Sound

| | | | | |
|---|---|---|---|---|
| are | start | star | carpet | starting |
| car | smart | are | farm | spark |
| bar | harp | harbor | harm | harming |
| tar | far | target | alarm | market |
| star | harm | carpet | jar | barking |
| jar | hark | parting | lark | parking |
| lark | market | are | park | darkest |
| park | parka | barking | mark | target |
| mark | cars | shark | darkest | starts |
| bark | jars | clark | dart | cards |
| dark | starts | starlit | card | stars |
| stark | parts | darkness | farm | parts |
| card | marks | parking | jar | barks |
| lard | stars | barking | are | far |
| dart | barks | smartest | par | harbor |

Do you think that a shark

Do

barks like a dog? Is it time

barks

to start playing the harp?

to

Are there stars far away in

A

the dark park? Are you afraid

the

of sharks in the dark?

# Lesson 27 – ee Sound

When two e's are next to each other, the sound is a long e, like in sleep.

| | | | | | |
|---|---|---|---|---|---|
| bee | feet | freed | meets | heel | green |
| see | meek | need | beets | keel | seek |
| fee | sheet | beef | feeds | see | seed |
| feed | meet | creep | teens | bee | deer |
| feel | seed | peep | seeks | meek | cheer |
| green | fleet | seek | cheek | keen | weed |
| screen | teeth | bleed | creek | seem | speed |
| deer | heed | seethe | feel | heed | creed |
| beer | weed | squeeze | bee | deed | freed |
| keen | deed | speeds | beer | seen | teen |
| teen | sweet | feels | meets | seem | feels |
| speed | weep | sees | green | tree | sheets |
| steep | keep | flee | three | | |
| three | teepee | seems | feet | | |
| seem | free | seen | beet | | |

Important Exception:

been sounds like

ben

98

There is a green monster whose

There

name is Pete. He has three

name

feet, three teeth, and he likes

feet

sweets a lot. He was last seen

sweets

sleeping in a tree. If you see Pete,

sleeping

do not feed him or squeeze him!

# Lesson 28 - When ea is Like ee

In a lot of words when "ea" is present, the letter a has to be quiet and let the letter e say it's name.

| | | | | |
|---|---|---|---|---|
| beat | team | beast | cream | squeaking |
| heat | each | squeak | eat | smearing |
| meat | beach | steam | peach | cheapest |
| treat | peach | please | tear | clearing |
| cream | veal | heap | fear | dearest |
| smear | eat | reap | clear | teardrop |
| hear | lean | leap | read | seating |
| tear | tea | treat | seat | speaking |
| fear | speak | clean | peach | heating |
| clear | yeast | near | cheap | stealing |
| near | seal | hear | reap | fearful |
| appear | peal | year | dear | beachball |
| cheap | dear | dear | clear | leapfrog |
| steal | east | rear | speak | teabag |
| spear | least | clear | peak | steamship |

Do you hear that leaping frog

Do

squeaking? Eat some meat,

squeaking

have a peach on the beach.

have

Please do not feed the beast

Please

a treat, dear. Can a seal speak,

a

can a beachball read?

# Lesson 29 - ei, ey & Long e Review

Sometimes when ei or ey are together, the i or y has to be quiet and let the e say it's name.

## ey, ei

money honey monkey donkey valley key
either neither money honey monkey

## Long e Review  - ( Some words have two meanings and two spellings.)

| | | | | | |
|---|---|---|---|---|---|
| he | leaf | heel | seen | feel | money |
| be | beam | peel | peach | keep | either |
| peas | bead | wheel | tree | need | key |
| teach | spear | sleep | here | sweet | keep |
| mean | wheat | speech | mere | green | beep |
| gear | zeal | breed | ear | hear | meat |
| dream | heat | steel | weep | year | dream |
| heal | near | steer | sleet | clear | steal |
| each | see | me | creep | sheep | please |
| weak | free | she | tea | sheet | scream |

Oh no, that bad monkey on a

Oh

donkey ate the whole pot of

donkey

honey ! Did she keep her sheep

honey

up in a tall tree ? Please do not

up

eat that green leaf for lunch !

eat

I was dreaming about a pig !

# Lesson 30 - Other ea, ey sounds

## ea, ey - long a sound (sometimes e has to be quiet & let a say its name, and sometimes ey sounds like ay)

great break wear bear pear tear
they hey prey grey obey convey
steak

## ea - short e sound (sometimes ea sounds like e as in wet.

head sweat spread tread health
dead read breath bread wealth
meant deaf death instead weapon
leather weather feather breakfast
ready heavy ( the y has a long e sound )

## ea - short a sound

heart sounds like hart

## ear - ur sound (sometimes ear makes an ur sound in a word.)

learn earth pearl heard search

That big black bear says that

That

he wants to eat a great big

he

steak for breakfast. Are you

steak

ready to spread some jelly on

ready

your bread? Does a pear have

your

feathers? Is a pearl heavy?

# Lesson 31 - ew, eu, eau, eye Sounds

<u>ew, eu - you sound</u> (sometimes words with ew or eu rhyme with you)
few    mew    pew    feud    view

<u>ew - long u sound</u>
new    drew    grew    jewel    strew    renew
blew    stew    crew    slew    threw    screw
dew    brew    mildew    withdrew    yew

<u>eau - you sound</u>
beauty    beautiful

<u>eau - long o sound</u>
plateau    bureau

<u>eye - long i sound</u>
eye

A bug blew into my eye.

Can a bug be beautiful? That

can

silly bear threw a jewel in

silly

my new meat stew! When

my

the green monster ate some

the

seeds, he grew and grew until

seeds,

he was bigger than the trees!

107

# Lesson 32 - Review of e sounds

## Short e sound (e, ea, ai)

| went | head | get | left | bread | head |
|------|------|-----|------|-------|------|
| fed | dead | met | meant | read | led |
| said | feather | yet | sweat | red | said |
| sent | spread | deaf | pet | bet | set |

## Long e sound (some of the words below mean two different things and can be spelled two ways.)

| hear | steal | meat | dear | see | week |
|------|-------|------|------|-----|------|
| here | steel | meet | deer | sea | weak |
| heel | peel | beet | seem | flee | teem |
| heal | peal | beat | seam | flea | team |
| read | beach | tea | here | he | be |
| reed | beech | tee | hear | me | she |

money honey key please sneeze ear

dream sheep beam sweet heat neat

cheerful smear cream peach teardrop

we he see bee she sleep clear either leaf

## Long a sound (ea, ey)

| | | | |
|---|---|---|---|
| great | prey | convey | grey |
| they | hey | break | obey |
| wear | tear | bear | prey |
| break | steak | pear | they |

## Long u, you sound (ew, eu, eau)

few   new   pew   yew   mew   crew
drew   feud   brew   threw   screw   stew
beautiful   blew   grew   few   withdrew

## Long o sound (eau)

plateau, bureau

## Long i sound (eye)

eye

Write some words below:

mew

109

# Lesson 33 - i, y Sounds

Most words with an ind or ild have a long i sound.

## ind, ild

| | | | | |
|---|---|---|---|---|
| wild | bind | child | kindness | kindest |
| mild | find | rind | binding | wildest |
| kind | blind | grind | mildest | finds |

Some exceptions are: **wind, children** which have a short i sound

## ie, y, ye  ie, y, ye have a long i sound in these words.

| | | | | |
|---|---|---|---|---|
| pie | pry | try | dies | fly |
| die | ply | shy | pies | cry |
| tie | spy | by | ties | my |
| rye | dry | sky | why | pie |
| why | fry | dry | my | rye |

Why do the children want to find my peach pie? Do not spy, my wild child. Try not to be shy, if you can fly.

Do you think that wild bears

Do

like to eat peach pie? He

like

is the kindest monster,

is

because he teaches me to fly

because

my kite in the wind. The sky

my

has a lot of stars in it!

# Lesson 34 - More i,y Sounds

## ie, ine, y - long e sound

| | | | |
|---|---|---|---|
| field | machine | happy | mommy |
| yield | magazine | carry | daddy |
| priest | ravine | hurry | story |
| believe | vaseline | daily | candy |

## ine, ive, ile, ite - short i sound (magic e exceptions)

| | | | |
|---|---|---|---|
| fragile | opposite | give live | ive |
| missile | favorite | attractive | expressive |
| medicine | imagine | engine | determine |

My mommy is happy when she gets time to read her favorite magazine.

I like it when my mommy or daddy reads me a story before I go to sleep. I believe I will give you some candy.

What is your very favorite

What

thing to do? Her mommy's

thing

favorite thing is to ride on

favorite

a donkey in a field while

a

reading a magazine and eating

reading

candy. Do you live in a tree?

113

# Lesson 35 – ir, er, ur, or, ear

All of these words have the ir sound that is in girl.

| ir | ur | ear | er |
|---|---|---|---|
| first | hurt | learn | her |
| girl | burn | search | herd |
| firm | hurl | yearn | perk |
| third | curl | earth | jerk |
| skirt | burst | heard | perch |
| birth | Thursday | pearl | fern |
| squirrel | murmur | | winter |
| whirl | curtain | **or** | summer |
| swirl | burden | word | teacher |
| sir | purr | work | sister |
| stir | blur | world | brother |
| shirt | flurry | worst | mother |
| squirt | fur | worth | father |
| squirm | surf | worse | quarter |

Can a squirrel wear a shirt,

Can

can a cat wear a skirt? One

can

hot summer Thursday, my

hot

brother made the worst, burnt

brother

dinner in the world! The red

dinner

bird sat on my teacher's ear.

115

# Lesson 36 - Long o Combinations

## OA (almost all the words with oa have a long o sound)

| | | | |
|---|---|---|---|
| boat | oak | moan | groan |
| coat | soak | bloat | toast |
| float | croak | goal | roast |
| moat | coal | boat | coast |
| road | oatmeal | coat | road |
| toad | gloat | toad | load |
| load | toast | load | moat |
| roast | groan | float | oats |

## o, oe (long o sound)

| | |
|---|---|
| go | no |
| no | lo |
| toe | so |
| foe | go |
| doe | toe |
| woe | foe |

## old, olt, oll (these have a long o sound)

| | | |
|---|---|---|
| old | bolt | toll |
| cold | colt | roll |
| told | jolt | poll |
| bold | fold | stroll |
| scold | gold | troll |
| mold | sold | cold |

on't - don't, won't

Sound-alike word:

comb

ost, oth

most

host

post, both

116

A cold old troll stole a boat

A

from a toad ! Don't scold

from

him for leaving his cold old

him

oatmeal in the road. Do you

oatmeal

have a coat made of gold ?

have

I told you not to eat that road!

# Lesson 37 - ow, oi, oy Sounds

## ow - long o sound (most of the time ow has a long o sound)

row   crow   bow   low   elbow   slow
glow   flow   show   blow   grow   mow
stow   window   meadow   fellow   hollow
pillow   shadow   shallow   below   grown
own

## ow - as in how (sometimes ow rhymes with cow)

how   now   allow   crowd   brown
bow   cow   chow   clown   frown
crown   drown   prowl   owl   fowl
growl   wow   vow   ow   pow   town

## oi, oy (these words all have the oy sound of toy.)

oil   coil   boy   enjoy   coin   joy   toy
coil   broil   toy   employ   oink   enjoy
boil   foil   joy   destroy   avoid   boil
spoil   soil   soy   annoy   boiler   coin

Show your elbow to a crow,
Show

throw your pillow out the
throw

window. Don't allow that
window

frowning clown to drown !
frowning

That boy enjoys playing with
That

his toy brown cow.

# Lesson 38 -ou Sounds (& ony off oss ost)

## ou - as in mouse, rhymes with now

house mouse ground pound founder
wound count ounce bounce pout our
about stout shout bout fountain hou
mount round around boundary out
loud cloud pound counter shouting

## ou - short u sound, rhymes with bun

cousin   young   trouble   double
couple   could   would   should
country  (could, would and should rhyme with book)
    touch

## ou - long u sound, rhymes with rule

group soup troupe route youth

## ou - aw sound  ost, off, ong oss - aw sound

your pour tour four court cost off
boss cross moss toss gloss floss loss
song along wrong long belong song

Could you hear that loud

Could

mouse bouncing around

mouse

the house ? Would your

the

young cousin get in trouble

young

if he found a monster in his

if

soup ? That's the wrong song.

121

# Lesson 39 -oo Sounds

## oo - long u sound, as in rule

| | | | | |
|---|---|---|---|---|
| broom | stool | troop | room | mood |
| boot | tool | droop | shoot | brood |
| loot | fool | stoop | pool | booth |
| toot | hoop | roof | food | tooth |
| moo | moon | spoon | noon | igloo |
| too | boo | spool | hoot | cool |
| | | | | zoo |

## oo - rhymes with wood

| | | | | |
|---|---|---|---|---|
| wood | took | crook | shook | cookie |
| book | cook | brook | hook | lookout |
| soot | look | hoof | book | footsteps |
| foot | nook | hood | look | cooking |
| good | stood | wool | rook | mistook |

## oo- aw sound
poor door floor

## oa -aw sound
roar soar

If you stood on a stool could

if

you touch the moon with a

you

broom ? Meet me at noon in

broom

the cool igloo and we will

the

eat some cookies with a spoon.

eat

I found a tooth in a book !

# Lesson 40 - Review of o sounds

| | | | | | |
|---|---|---|---|---|---|
| or | toy | work | cool | four | soup |
| corn | joy | word | tool | young | group |
| born | oil | come | cook | trouble | pour |
| bore | cow | some | book | double | poor |
| top | now | shop | hood | loud | door |
| cop | pow | chop | took | cloud | floor |
| cope | allow | to | coal | proud | tour |
| mope | below | do | goal | hour | zoo |
| hope | grow | no | pole | flour | boot |
| on | sow | go | cole | sour | loot |
| gone | crow | does | born | our | smooth |
| old | glow | wood | horn | sound | root |
| cold | clown | would | chore | mound | scoop |
| troll | loaf | could | core | town | boom |
| fold | alone | boot | foot | crown | good |
| foe | boy | food | wool | own | hood |

Do cows say moo? Was that

Do

old monkey a lot of trouble?

old

Does that cold troll glow in

Does

the dark? Don't make a

the

sound, go and hide in the

sound,

ground. Don't eat the sour soup.

# Lesson 41 - u Sounds

## ue, ui, u - long u sound

| | | | | | |
|---|---|---|---|---|---|
| sue | value | suit | truth | duel | true |
| blue | true | fruit | tune | fuel | truth |
| clue | blue | juice | rule | value | fruit |
| true | clue | suit | cruel | clue | suit |

## ui - short i sound

build  building built builder
guilt  guilty quilt quit quick

## u - same sound as in wood

put  pull  bull  full  pudding
pulling  bullfrog  fuller (would, could, should)

Tell me the truth. Where did you put the fruitjuice and the blue pudding? I bet you gave them to the bullfrog.

Please drink your blue juice

Please

quickly. Is it true that there

quickly

is a big bull in that building?

is

Quit eating all the blue fruit!

Quit

It is cruel to have a duel.

It

Follow the rule, ride on a mule.

Have you ever heard an owl

Have

growl ? Does a cow say moo,

growl

and a cat say mew ? Is it

and

true that Sue saw a mouse

true

with a blue suit on ? Put that

with

poor cow on the roof !

# Chapter 5.

Lessons 42 - 60

Silent Letters
Other Consonant Sounds
Endings
Contractions
Common Exceptions
Important Words to Know
Numbers
500 Most Common Words

# Lesson 42 - Silent Letters (k, g, w, b)

In some words when there are two consonant sounds together, one of them has to be quiet and let the other make its normal sound. (Silent letters are made here with dotted lines.)

**kn** (sounds like n)

knife
knit
knack
know
knapsack
knob
knuckle
knew
known
kneel
knelt

**gn** (sounds like n)

gnat
gnaw
sign
gnash
gnome
gnarl

**bt** (sounds like t)

debt
doubt

**mb** (sounds like m)

comb
bomb
numb
dumb
limb
crumb
climb
thumb

**wr** (sounds like r)

write wrench wrap wrist
wreath wretched wreck
writing wrestle written

130

Does that silly gnome know

Does

that his knapsack is full of

that

crumbs? Does a cat know

crumbs

how to read and write?

how

I saw that gnome gnashing

i

his teeth, I know it!

131

# Lesson 43 - Silent Letters (w, p, n, h, l)

**sw** (sounds like s)

answer

**pn** (sounds like n)

pneumonia

**ho, oh** (sounds like short or long o)

hour
honor
honest
ghost
John
oh
Thomas

**ps** (sounds like s)

psalm

**mn** (sounds like m)

hymn
column

**rh** (sounds like r)

rhyme
rhythm

**lm, ld, lf, lk** (l is silent)

"ah" sound {
calm
palm
psalm
balmy
}

"short a" sound {
calf
half
}

would
should
could
} rhymes with good

balk
talk
walk
} "awk" sound

folk
polka
yolk
} "oke" sound

132

Would you be calm if you saw

Would

a ghost ? Can ghosts walk

a

or talk, or sing hymns like

or

Tim ? Answer me honestly,

Tim

would you ride on a calf or

would

split a brick in half ?

# Lesson 44 - Silent Letters -gh

Most of the time when gh is in a word, <u>both</u> letters are silent

## ight - sounds like ite

fight  tight  flight  night  slight
night  right  fright  light  mighty
might  sight  bright  thigh  sigh

## aigh, eigh - long a sound

straight  eight  weigh  weight  freight
sleigh  neighbor  eighteen  eighty

## augh, ough - "aw" sound

caught  naughty  bought  sought
taught  slaughter  fought  thought
brought

## ough - "ew" sound
through

## ough - long o sound

dough  doughnut  though  although

134

Eighteen neighbors saw a

Eighteen

bright light right in the

bright

middle of the night ! Have

middle

you ever thought about being

you

naughty and eating eighty

naughty

big doughnuts in a row ?

# Lesson 45 - Other ph, gh, ch Sounds

When there is a ph in a word it has an f sound. In some words, gh also sounds like f.

## ph - f sound

phone
photograph
telephone
orphan
alphabet
elephant

## gh - f sound

laugh } short a sound

enough
rough } rhymes with puff
tough

cough ("aw" sound)

## ch - k sound (sometimes ch sounds like k)

Christian
Christmas
orchid
ache
chemical
school

## ch - sh sound (sometimes ch sounds like sh)

Chicago
chef
chevy
Michigan
Michelle
machine

Can an elephant learn the

Can

alphabet ? Don't laugh,

alphabet

that elephant asked for a

that

photograph of a telephone

photograph

for Christmas ! Did that

for

rough old troll go to school ?

# Lesson 46 - Soft c, g & dge

When c comes before i, e, or y is usually has a soft sound, like s.
When a word ends in nce, the vowel before the n is usually short.

| ce | ci | cy | nce |
|---|---|---|---|
| face | city | cycle | dance |
| rice | pencil | mercy | prance |
| nice | cider | bicycle | mince |
| race | civil | cymbal | since |
| price | | fancy | chance |
| cent | | | lance |
| | | | silence |
| | | | prince |

## gi, gy, ge, dge

Sometimes g sounds like j, and this usually happens in gi, gy, ge. dge also sounds like j.

| gi | gy | ge | dge |
|---|---|---|---|
| ginger | gym | urge | edge |
| magic | gypsy | rage | fudge |
| rigid | stingy | agent | bridge |
| frigid | | wage | smudge |
| | | gem | |

## Some exceptions to soft g are:

give      girl      gear      get

giggle    finger    geese     gift

gilt      gist      given     girl

Do you think there is a chance that the nice old gypsy can turn my bicycle into a piece of fudge by magic? It is your last chance to dance on the bridge with the nice mice! The prince flew into a rage when they put him in a cage.

# Lesson 47 - z,s Sounds

When s is followed by a consonant it is usually soft. When s is followed by e or y at the end of a word, it usually has a z sound.

## When s sounds like z, z words

| | | | |
|---|---|---|---|
| wise | rise | maze | blaze |
| close | tease | craze | glaze |
| rose | pansy | crazy | daze |
| cheese | choose | lazy | amaze |
| please | raise | excuse | craze |
| vase | rouse | haze | ablaze |
| phase | ease | hazy | gaze |
| those | easy | graze | size |
| these | busy | frozen | prize |
| hose | business | size | apologize |
| noise | raisin | amaze | froze |
| poison | arise | daze | doze |
| nose | | | |

Important exceptions: (s still has soft sound)

loose, moose, noose, house, mouse, louse

Were you amazed at the size

*Were*

of those frozen roses?

*of*

Please excuse him for acting

*Please*

crazy and lazy. Is it wise

*crazy*

to put a raisin on your nose?

*to*

Please don't eat that pansy!

# Lesson 48 - Sounds of: cia, cious, tious, xious, tion, sion, su, ture

Sometimes the endings tion, cia, cious, xious, and tious have a shu sound

## tion, tien | cia, cious, xious, sion

action     special     anxious

nation     social     mansion

mention     vicious     pension

vacation     cautious     permission

patient     delicious     admission

attention     suspicious     expression

fiction     gracious

fraction     precious     ture - sounds like chore

question     nature

picture, mixture

Sometimes sion on the end of a word sounds like it does in "television" and su sounds the same.

television     usual     treasure

vision     usually     measure

precision     decision     version

Would a mixture of frog's

Would

teeth and bat's tails taste

teeth

very delicious? Would you

very

be anxious if you had to

be

sleep in a haunted mansion

sleep

on your next vacation?

# Lesson 49 - le, ly Sounds

le - sounds like l, the e is silent.

| | | | |
|---|---|---|---|
| tickle | puzzle | able | fable |
| cuddle | snuggle | cripple | sparkle |
| muddle | bubble | apple | poodle |
| huddle | ankle | double | tinkle |
| jungle | table | trouble | oodle |
| grizzle | stable | single | maple |
| sizzle | cradle | crackle | dazzle |
| riddle | fiddle | cable | beetle |
| noodle | people | pebble | wiggle |
| thimble | eagle | tremble | dangle |
| knuckle | beagle | shuttle | couple |
| hobble | bible | muffle | ample |
| cobble | circle | candle | castle |
| little | kettle | sparkle | title |
| brittle | settle | muscle | bugle |

## ly (sounds like lee)

| | | | |
|---|---|---|---|
| wisely | freely | mostly | purely |
| surely | quickly | safely | lately |
| lovely | slowly | lately | blindly |
| badly | sadly | ghostly | pebbly |
| nearly | yearly | hardly | ugly |

You will get in trouble if you feed that ugly grizzly bear oodles of noodles!

That little beetle was nearly eaten by an eagle.

Could an apple be inside a bubble?

Who was playing that bugle in the jungle?

Don't wiggle, or I'll tickle you under the table in the stable!

# Lesson 50 - Endings (ies, ied, ier, iest)

Many words that end in y need to change to ies for their plural form, and to ied for their past tense.

## y - ies, ied (ie keeps long e sound of y)

party - parties    berry - berries
fairy - fairies    baby - babies
lady - ladies    story - stories
carry - carries    hurry - hurries
bunny - bunnies    penny - pennies
hurry - hurried    carry - carried

## y - ier, iest (the y changes to an i but keeps the long e sound, and the er or est has its normal sound)

happy - happier - happiest
lucky - luckier - luckiest
ugly - uglier - ugliest
funny - funnier - funniest
shady - shadier - shadiest
thirsty - thirstier - thirstiest
sleepy - sleepier - sleepiest

Those are the luckiest baby

Those

bunnies! Those fairies gave

bunnies

them all the blueberries in

them

the forest! That fairy told

the

the silliest stories I ever

the

heard!

# Lesson 51 - ing Endings

In some cases, you need to double the last consonant of a word when adding ing.

hop - hopping     whip - whipping

beg - begging     sled - sledding

grab - grabbing     trip - tripping

bet - betting     nag - nagging

tap - tapping.     tug - tugging

skip - skipping     drip - dripping

slip - slipping     spin - spinning

All the words above have short vowels, and the double consonants before ing tell you that the first vowel is still short.
In words with long vowels and magic e at the end, take away the magic e before adding ing.

fire - firing     care - caring

skate - skating     stare - staring

name - naming     tape - taping

hope - hoping     make - making

bake - baking     rake - raking

save - saving     freeze - freezing

sneeze - sneezing     hide - hiding
please - pleasing     smile - smiling
leave - leaving       time - timing
shine - shining       drive - driving
slide - sliding       wire - wiring
swipe - swiping       ride - riding
dine - dining         flame - flaming

Most other words which have vowel combinations, and end in one or two consonants do not change before adding ing.

lick - licking        start - starting
stick - sticking      feed - feeding
fail - failing        roast - roasting
head - heading        stand - standing
kneel - kneeling      oil - oiling
feel - feeling        hear - hearing
read - reading        steal - stealing
look - looking        out - outing

# Lesson 52 - ed, en Endings

Most of the time the e in the ed ending is silent, and just the d is pronounced. Just the same as when ing is added, some words need to double their consonants to remind you of their short vowel sound. Many words stay the same before adding ed, and those which already end in e just add a d.

## ed

| | | |
|---|---|---|
| robbed | jogged | learned |
| sobbed | topped | called |
| flopped | fretted | loved |
| mopped | kissed | saved |
| crossed | chimed | lived |
| tossed | chipped | chased |
| liked | licked | fired |
| smiled | smelled | striped |

## en

The same rules apply to words ending with en, but en always rhymes w

| | | |
|---|---|---|
| chosen | lighten | risen |
| frozen | brighten | beaten |
| broken | loosen | eaten |
| quicken | darken | fallen |

A goose chased a wild moose.

The chicken was chosen to

be frozen. I liked that

smiling old troll whose pinky

was broken. Have you ever

kissed a cat or a bat?

151

# Lesson 53 - Contractions

Sometimes two words combine into one and have an apostrophe in between.

| | |
|---|---|
| cannot | - can't |
| do not | - don't |
| have not | - haven't |
| does not | - doesn't |
| will not | won't |
| did not | didn't |
| could not | couldn't |
| should not | shouldn't |
| would not | wouldn't |
| had not | hadn't |
| was not | wasn't |
| is not | isn't |
| it is | it's |

An apostrophe is also used to indicate that a thing belongs to someone.

Ann's coat
Dad's knife
Ted's kite
Lisa's pig
John's cat

a cat's hat
the rat's mat
the pig's wig
the fool's stool
the man's fan

It's great that Ann's goat wasn't outside when it snowed.

you shouldn't say that he

you

doesn't like eating spiders!

doesn't

wouldn't that silly little

wouldn't

gnome go home? I don't know

gnome

if that red hen's eggs are wet,

if

she won't let me look.

# Lesson 54-Review-Exceptions

These words sound differently than they are spelled.

The magic e rule is broken in these words:

| | | | |
|---|---|---|---|
| gone | done | one | come |
| some | become | are | have |
| give | were | love | glove |
| above | there | where | |

These words have a long u sound

| | | | |
|---|---|---|---|
| you | two | who | do |
| to | | | |

In these words su sounds like sh

| | | |
|---|---|---|
| sure | surely | sugar |

These words have vowel sounds that are unexpected:

| | | | |
|---|---|---|---|
| been | of | once | does |
| was | heart | idea | said |
| again | against | dog | says |

Do you two love the idea of

eating some grasshoppers

with sugar on top ? He said

that he had been dreaming

about flying above the trees

again !

# Lesson 55 - Review - Words that sound alike & Words that are spelled alike

Some words sound the same but are spelled differently and have different meanings:

maid, made          steak, stake

bear, bare          break, brake

pray, prey          wear, ware

pair, pear,         stair, stare

pail, pale          steel, steal

peel, peal          reel, real

mail, male          heal, heel

Other words can be pronounced two different ways to mean two different things:

tear     (can sound like teer or tare)

read     (can sound like reed or red)

lead     (can sound like leed or led)

bow      (can sound like bow or boe)

live     (can sound like liv or live)

Is that big bear bare? Please

is

send a pair of pears to a

send

male cat through the mail.

male

Can a monkey wearing a

Can

black bow-tie steal a steak

black

or read a good book?

# Lesson 56 – Important Words

## Days, Months, Seasons

| | | |
|---|---|---|
| Sunday | January | August |
| Monday | February | September |
| Tuesday | March | October |
| Wednesday | April | November |
| Thursday | May | December |
| Friday | June | winter, spring |
| Saturday | July | summer, fall |

## People

| | | Food |
|---|---|---|
| mother | grandmother | cake |
| father | grandfather | cookie |
| sister | babysitter | cereal |
| brother | teacher | carrots |
| aunt | step-sister | vegetables |
| uncle | friend | spaghetti |
| cousin | parent | pudding |

Did your grandmother let you

Did

eat spaghetti and cookies

eat

that rainy Thursday morning

that

in September ? Did your

in

mother see a monster one

mother

Monday morning in March ?

# Lesson 57 – Numbers

| | | | | |
|---|---|---|---|---|
| 1 - One | 17 - seventeen | first |
| 2 two | 18 - eighteen | second |
| 3 three | 19 - nineteen | third |
| 4 four | 20 twenty | fourth |
| 5 five | 30 thirty | fifth |
| 6 six | 40 forty | sixth |
| 7 seven | 50 fifty | seventh |
| 8 eight | 60 sixty | eighth |
| 9 nine | 70 seventy | ninth |
| 10 ten | 80 eighty | tenth |
| 11 eleven | 90 ninety | |
| 12 twelve | 100 one hundred | |
| 13 thirteen | 1000 one thousand | |
| 14 fourteen | 1,000,000 one million | |
| 15 fifteen | | |
| 16 sixteen | | |

1 1 2 2 3 3 4 4 5 5 6 6 7 7
8 8 9 9 10 10

Was it the second time

Was

that you saw a million

that

elephants eating eighty

elephants

easter eggs each ?

easter

# Lesson 58 – Most Common Words

a about above across act add after again against already also always am America American among an and another answer any anything appear are arm around as ask at away

back bank be became because become been before began begin being believe best better between big bill body book both boy bring brought built business but by

call came can car care carry case cause chance change child children city close color come coming company condition consider continue cost cut could country course court cover cry

day dear demand did die different do
doctor does dollar done don't door
down dress drop during

each early either end enough even
evening ever every everything eye

face fact fall family far father fear
feel feet felt few fight figure fill
find fine fire first five follow food
for force found four friend from
front full

garden gave get girl give given go God
gone good got government great green

had half hand happen happy hard
has have he head hear heard heart
held help her here herself high him

# Lesson 59 - Common Words Continued

himself his hold home hope horse
hour house how however human
hundred husband

I idea if I'll important in increase
interest into is it its itself

John just

keep kept kind ring knew know

labor lady land large last late laugh
law learn least leave left less let
letter lie life light like line little live
long look lost love low

made make man many mark marry
matter may me mean men might mile
mind miss moment money month more

morning most mother move Mr. Mrs. much must my myself

name national near need never new New York next night no nor not note nothing now number

of off office often old on once one only open or other our out over own

paper part party pass pay people perhaps person picture place plan put plant play point poor possible power present president price produce public

question quite quiet quick quit

rather reach read real reason recieve red remain remember rest result

# Lesson 60 - Common Words Continued

return right river road room round run

said same sat saw say school sea second
see seem seen serve set several shall she
ship short should show side since sir
small smile so some something son
soon sort sound speak stand start state
step still stood stop story street strong
such sun supply suppose sure system

table take taken talk tell ten than that
the their them themselves then there
they thing think this those though
thought thousand three through thus
time to today together told too took
toward town tree tried true try turn
twenty two

under until up upon us use

very voice

wait walk wall want war was
Washington watch water way we
week well went were what when
where whether which while white
who whole whom whose why wife
will wind window wish with within
without woman women wonder word
work world would write wrong

year yes yet you young your

Do you believe that three

thousand children were

standing on their heads in

the great green garden this

morning ? The president

herself saw them do it !

# Chapter 6.

# Handwriting Practice

# Some of the Different Ways Italic Can Look

Everyone has their own favorite way of writing in Italic. Some people prefer to continue writing an upright style, like this. Many left-handers feel most comfortable with upright Italic.

It is also possible to write a somewhat faster version of upright Italic. In this case, the letters will join each other sometimes, just as they do in fast slanted Italic writing.

Most right handers and many left handers feel more comfortable with a slanted Italic. You may decide to write without joining any letters, or only a very few, if you wish. It will be just a little slower to write with no joins, but will be very easy to read.

If you write faster, some of your letters will join each other. If you closely follow the suggestions on joining in the coming pages of this chapter, you'll find that some of your words will have no joins, and most will have one or two. Remember to use joins only where they naturally occur... too many joins makes your writing harder to read. Also try not to write so quickly that your letters begin to deteriorate and become too hard to read.

Some people like to make their letters very wide, like this. You can try making your letters like this if you especially like the way it looks.

Other people like to write especially narrow letters. You can make your letters extra wide or extra narrow if you wish, but it will make your writing a bit harder to read if you do.

Some people prefer to write with an edged pen at all times. You can write slowly and carefully with an edged pen if you are writing something that is very important.

However, you may also write very quickly with an edged pen, allowing some of your letters to join together. Your fast writing with the edged pen may not look quite as beautiful to you as your slow writing, but it still will look nice in it's own way!

## Using This Chapter

The previous pages give you an idea of some of the different ways that Italic handwriting can look, and how a progression can be made from a simple, upright version to a fast, semi-joined version done with a calligraphy pen.

Make sure that you have read over the section called "About Writing", in Chapter One, and gone over the basic Italic letters in Chapter Two before using this chapter. As well, spend some time practicing writing in the large size that is used throughout the sixty lessons.

In this chapter, you will start off writing simple upright Italic letters in a slightly smaller size. Trace and copy the six pages of the poem "The Night Before Christmas." Then try to do some additional writing practice on your own. Or, if you prefer, go directly to the next step, which will be writing these same letters with a slight slant to the right. Finish tracing and copying the poem in this slanted version of Italic, and then do some more practice on your own.

The next step is to begin writing slanted Italic in a slightly smaller size, one which corresponds to the size most adults use for normal handwriting. Find the size that feels most comfortable to *you* and continue to practice writing unjoined letters in this size.

Then, you will be ready to learn how to join some of the letters together so that you may write a fast version of Italic. Finally, you will have the option of learning to write both fast and slow versions of Italic with a calligraphy pen. This will make writing even more fun to do and beautiful to look at.

Most people can easily master the basics of Italic handwriting, as presented here, within a matter of a few weeks with daily practice. You should go through the different stages at whatever pace feels right to you, though, whether it takes one week or several months.

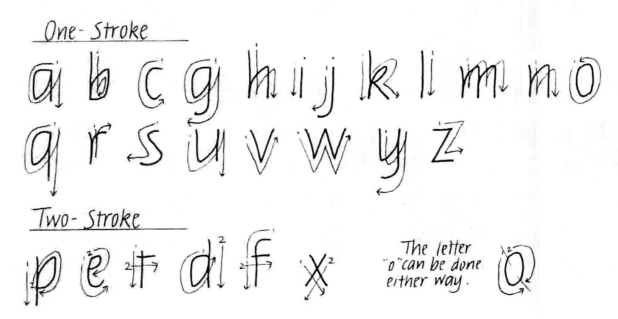

172

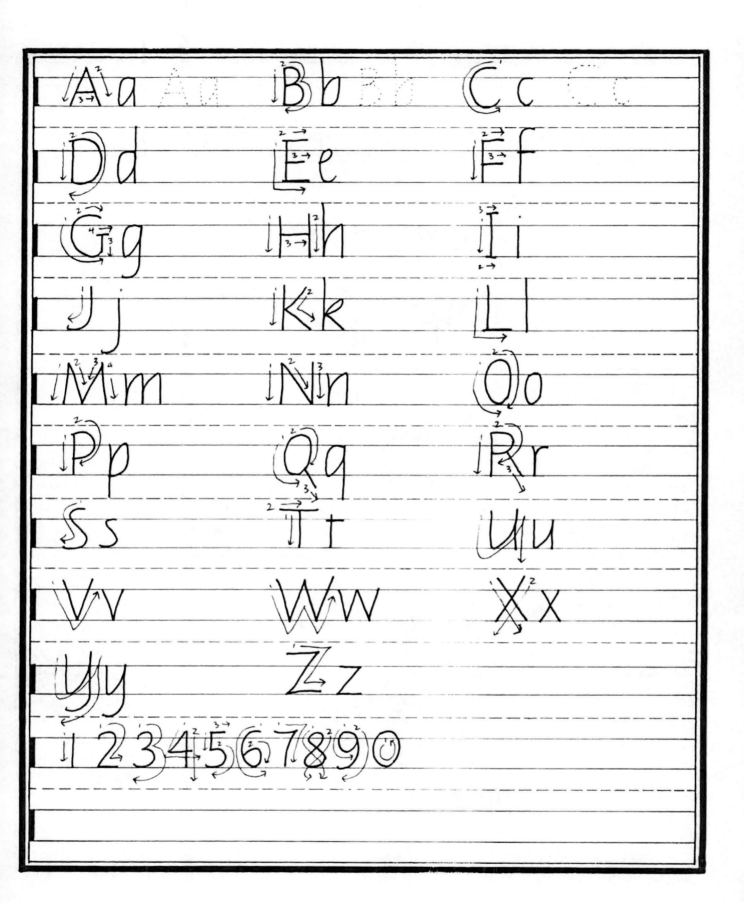

173

## The Night Before Christmas

'Twas the night before Christmas,

When all through the house,

Not a creature was stirring,

not even a mouse. The stockings

were hung by the chimney with

care, In hopes that St. Nicholas

soon would be there.

The children were nestled all snug

in their beds, While visions of

sugarplums danced in their heads.

And Mamma in her kerchief and

I in my cap had just settled down

for a long winter's nap.

When out on the lawn there

arose such a clatter, I sprang

from my bed to see what was the

from

matter. Away to the window I flew

matter

like a flash, tore open the shutters,

like

and threw up the sash. The moon

and

on the breast of the new-fallen

on

snow gave a luster of midday to

snow

objects below. When what to my

objects

wondering eyes should appear, but

wondering

176

a miniature sleigh, and eight tiny

a

reindeer. With a little old driver, so

reindeer

lively and quick, I knew in a

lively

moment it must be St. Nick.

moment

More rapid than eagles his coursers

More

they came. And he whistled, and

they

shouted, and called them by name:

shouted

"Now, Dasher! Now Dancer!

Now

Now Prancer and Vixen! On,

Now

Comet! On, Cupid! On Donder

Comet

and Blitzen! To the top of the

and

porch, to the top of the wall! Now,

porch

dash away! Dash away! Dash

dash

away all!"

away

As dry leaves that before the

As

wild hurricane fly, when they

wild

meet with an obstacle, mount to

meet

the sky. So up to the housetop the

coursers they flew, with a sleigh full

of toys, and St. Nicholas, too.

And then in a twinkling, I heard

on the roof, the prancing and

pawing of each little hoof. As I

drew in my head, and was turning

around, down the chimney St.

Nicholas came with a bound.

179

# Slanted Letters

There is another way to make the letters, and that is to slant them. When you write quickly, your letters will normally slant to the right. Continue copying the poem with the slanted letters.

## Straight Letters

abcdefghijklmnopqrstuv
wxyz  ABCDEFGHIJKL
MNOPQRSTUVWXYZ

## Slanted Letters

abcdefghijklmnop
qrstuvwxyz

ABCDEFGHIJKLMN
OPQRSTUVWXYZ

1 2 3 4 5 6 7 8 9 0

The lines on the following pages show you how much to slant the letters: *hill*

He was dressed all in fur, from

his head to his foot, and his clothes

were all tarnished with ashes and

soot. A bundle of toys he had flung

on his back, and he looked like a

peddler just opening his pack.

His eyes how they twinkled ! His

dimples how merry ! His cheeks

were like roses, his nose like a cherry.

*were*

His droll little mouth was drawn up

*His*

like a bow, and the beard on his chin

*like*

was as white as the snow. The stump

*was*

of a pipe he held in his teeth, and the

*of*

smoke, it encircled his head like a

*smoke*

wreath. He had a broad face and a

*wreath*

little round belly, that shook when

*little*

182

he laughed like a bowl full of jelly.

He was chubby and plump, a right

jolly old elf, and I laughed when I

saw him in spite of myself. A wink

of his eye and a twist of his head

soon gave me to know I had nothing

to dread. He spoke not a word, but

went straight to his work, and filled

183

all the stockings, then turned with

a jerk. And laying his finger aside

of his nose, and giving a nod, up the

chimney he rose. He sprang to his

sleigh, to his team gave a whistle,

and away they all flew like the

down of a thistle. But I heard him

exclaim as he drove out of sight,

"Happy Christmas to all and to
*Happy*
all a good night!"
*all*

The End
*The End*

Trace, copy, and finish these sentences.

My name is

I live

I love to

I hate to

My favorite food is

My favorite holiday is

If I could, I would

186

Use this page to write a funny story, or to practice writing anything you wish.

Most people end up writing in about this size. If you use regular notebook paper to write on, there will not be any slant lines, but you will naturally slant your letters once you have practiced a lot. Use the bottom line for your letters to rest on. Try to keep your letters as even as you can at the top also. Trace over this page and copy it below also.

Jack and Jill went up the hill
Jack
To fetch a pail of water
To
Jack fell down and broke his crown
Jack
And Jill came tumbling after.
And

Jack Sprat will eat no fat

His wife will eat no lean

And so between the two of them

They licked the platter clean.

Use this page to practice writing smaller.

# Joining Letters Together

In order to write quickly it is a good idea to allow some of the letters to join together. Some letters will need to change a little bit in order for this to happen smoothly.

These letters will stay the same.

# b c e f g i j o p q r s t v w x y

These letters will change a bit. At the end of the letter, continue coming up just a little bit to the right.

# a h k l m n d u z

The most important thing of all is that your writing always be very easy for other people to read, as *well* as being fast to write. Too many joins between letters, especially those made by loops, make your handwriting hard to read. Also, it is *slower to write* in a legible way when all the letters are joining.

Some letters should join each other, then, and others should not. Joining should occur naturally, and never be forced or done in an awkward manner simply for its own sake. If you follow the basic guidelines provided here for joining, as well as your own instincts, you will acquire a pleasant looking version of fast Italic within a short time. Trace over the joining combinations shown here as well as the quotations on the following pages, and then copy them. This will give you a good understanding of the way joins should be used. Notice that some of the words written on these pages have no joins in them, while others have one or two. It is not necessary to make joins on *every* possible occasion. If you wish to write with very few joins, in fact, it will take just a *little* bit longer to write. The fewer joins, the more legible your writing will be.

## Joining Guidelines

Do not make joins *from* the letters *g, y, j, q, p* or *f*. If you do, loops will be formed, which will make your writing harder to read. Also, do not make joins from the letters *b* or *r*, because these will tend to distort the letter shapes and make them hard to read.

*grow yes jot quill pray fit     bring     reason*

Do not make joins *into* the letters *b, l, h, k*, or *f*. If you do, loops are likely to form here also. As well, do not join into the letters *a, c, g, d*, or *s*. If you do, these letters will tend to become unattractive as well as hard to read.

*mob ill ah back if     mut ace pig add is*

190

# Possible Joins

ai ae an am ap ar au ay aj   ce ci cu cy ct

de di du dy dr do     hi he ho hu hy

ke ki ko ky   le li lo lp lt ly   me mi mo mu my

ne ni no np nu ny   ze zi zo zy   si se su sy

ta te ti tr to tt tu ty   fa fe fi fu fl ff ft fy fr fo

Some people like to join from o, v, and w :

oo oi on om ou oy oe    vi ve vy wi we wo

191

# Joining Practice

Friendships are fragile things and require as much care in handling as any other fragile thing.

It is a beautiful necessity of our nature to love something.                    Jerrold

A good book is the best of friends, the same today and forever                    Tupper

It is not how much we have but how much we enjoy that makes happiness                    Spurgeon

Insomuch as love grows in you so beauty grows, for love is the beauty of the soul.          St. Augustine


To live is not to live for one's self alone; let us help one another.                          Menander


We have been born to associate with our fellow-men, and to join in community with the human race.  Cicero


He who loses wealth loses much; he who loses a friend loses much more; but he who loses his courage loses all.
                                                          Cervantes

A man's true wealth is the good he does in this world.     Mohammed

The equal right of all men to the use of land is as clear as their equal right to breathe the air — it is a right proclaimed by the fact of their existence. For we cannot suppose that some men have a right to be in this world and others no right.     H. George

They who forgive most shall be most forgiven.  Bailey

Gentleness succeeds better than violence. La Fontaine

He who has health has hope, and he who has hope has everything.          Arabian proverb

There is no grief which time does not lesson and soften.          Cicero

There is nothing so powerful as truth; and often nothing so strange.          Daniel Webster

Whatever you can do or dream you can, begin it - for boldness has genius, power, and magic in it.          Goethe

# Using the Edged Pen

Your basic Italic writing will look even more beautiful if you use a "calligraphy" or "edged" pen to write with. Instead of coming to a point like a regular pen or pencil, an edged pen has an edge on it. The exact width of that edge (also called a "nib") will determine the size and thickness of your letters.

There are several different types of edged pens available. The three major types are magic marker calligraphy pens, fountain pens, and dip pens.

Magic marker edged pens are the easiest to use. They come in different sizes and colors, and are often available in stationery stores and sometimes even in large supermarkets. This is the kind of pen that you should get to start out with, if you can. Try to get one that is close to the size of the model letters on the facing page.

Another type of edged pen is a fountain pen, which has an ink-filled cartridge inside the pen. You can get different nibs for these pens, to use for writing in various sizes. The Shaeffer brand of fountain pen is the easiest to use. If you can get one of these, you will find that the fine and medium nibs will be very useful for this chapter.

A third type of edged pen is called a dip pen, which means that you must continually dip the metal nib into a bottle of ink as you are writing. These are the pens used by professional calligraphers. Since they are difficult to use, however, it is best to wait until you are more experienced before trying them.

The same pen can make thick short letters, regular size letters, or very tall and skinny letters. If you make your letters about five times as high as your pen nib's width it will look just right. If letters are too fat or too skinny, they may be harder to read and less beautiful.

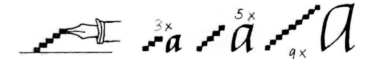

One reason that writing with an edged pen looks more attractive is that some parts of the letters are thicker than others. However, in order to make the *right* parts of the letter thin or thick, it is important to hold the pen at a certain angle. The dotted diagonal lines across the pages in this section of the book show you the angle at which to hold your pen. This may be difficult at first, but you will get the hang of it with practice. If you hold your pen at the wrong angle, the letters may end up looking too pointed and spiky or too flat and thick.

Make sure that you don't press too hard on the pen . . . but do be sure that the *entire edge* of the pen is pressed against the paper at all times. If it isn't, your letters may look scratchy and ragged.

Make photocopies of the pages with ruled lines, so that you can practice on them. Also, you can put thin white typing paper over them and the lines will show through. This is the best way to write poems, letters, etc. without having to use lined paper.

196

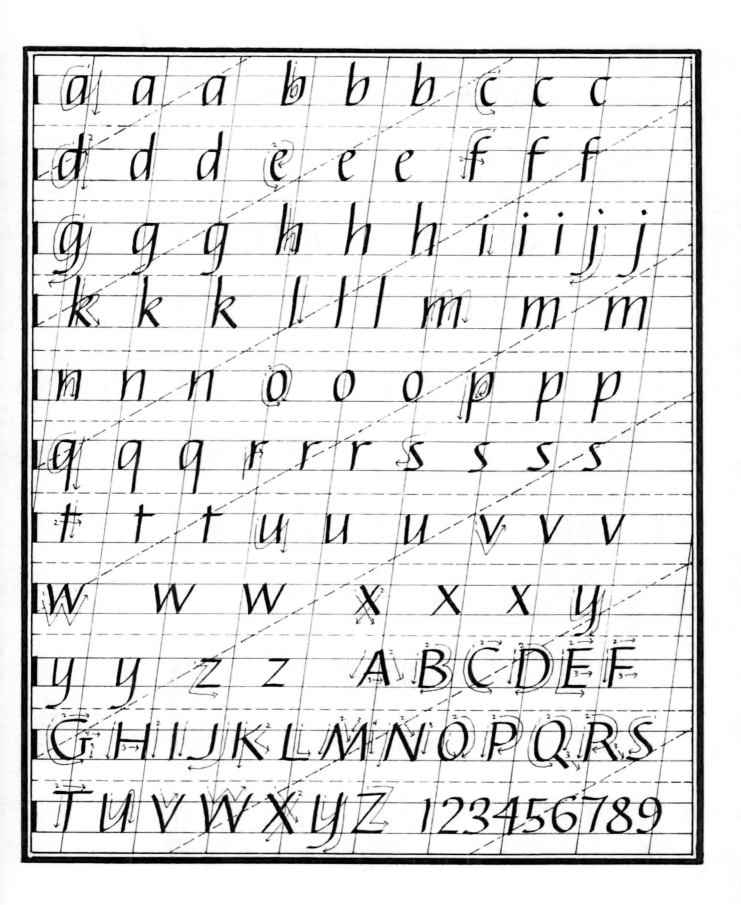

True ease in writing comes

from art, not chance, as

those move easiest who have

learned to dance.    A. Pope

Life is a flower, of which

love is the honey.

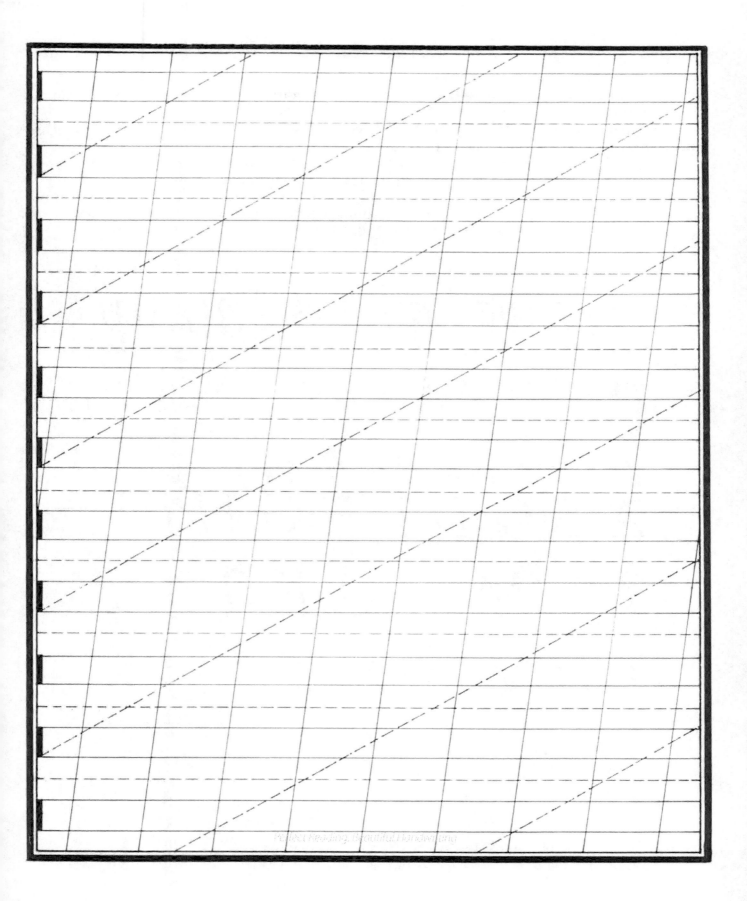

199

## Adding Serifs

Now you are going to start making the letters look just a little more "finished." You will be adding "serifs", or *very short* beginning and ending strokes to your letters, as shown. Continue to keep checking to see that you are holding your pen at the right angle. Try to see to it that your letters are slanted consistently as well. Also, try to keep most of the letters very close to the same width.

In order to be sure that you don't get your ascenders (top parts of *f, h, l, k, b*) and descenders (bottom parts of *f, g, j, q, p, y*) tangled up together, write on every *third* line only.

Trace and then copy the letters on this page and the quotations on the following pages. Then practice writing on your own, using this new version of Italic with serifs.

a b c d e f g h i j k l m n o p

q r s t u v w x y z  (Note that f and p look different now)

Capitals with Serifs

A B C D E F G H I J

K L M N O P Q R S

T U V W X Y Z

Small letters are best done at this 30° angle.

Capital letters, however, do look better when the pen is slightly flatter.

When adding serifs to capitals, the pen needs to be at a flatter angle, as shown here.

200

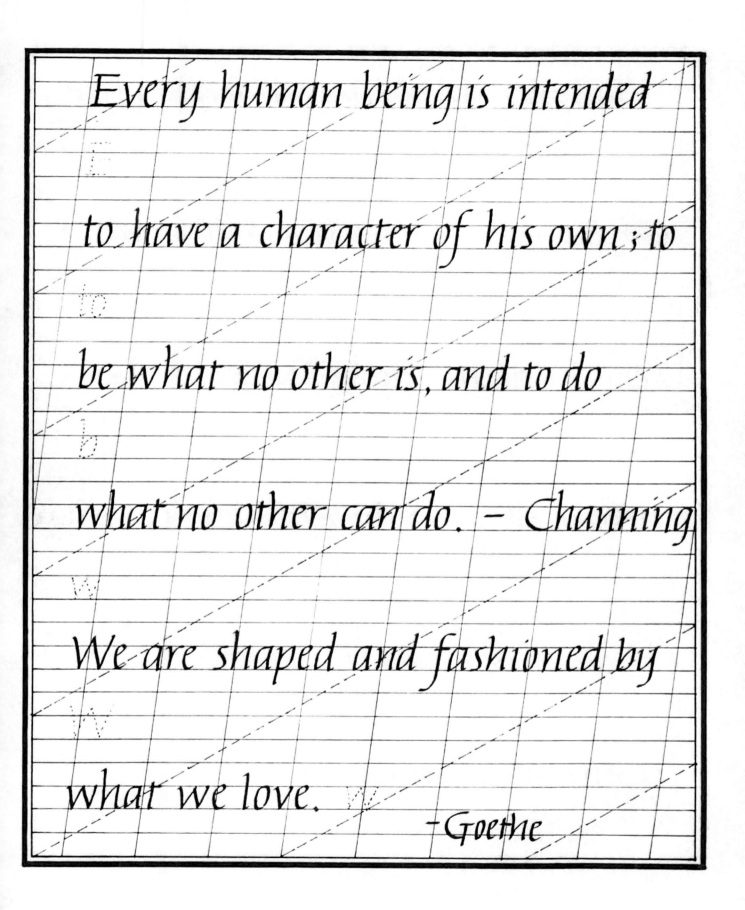

Every human being is intended

to have a character of his own; to

be what no other is, and to do

what no other can do. – Channing

We are shaped and fashioned by

what we love.

—Goethe

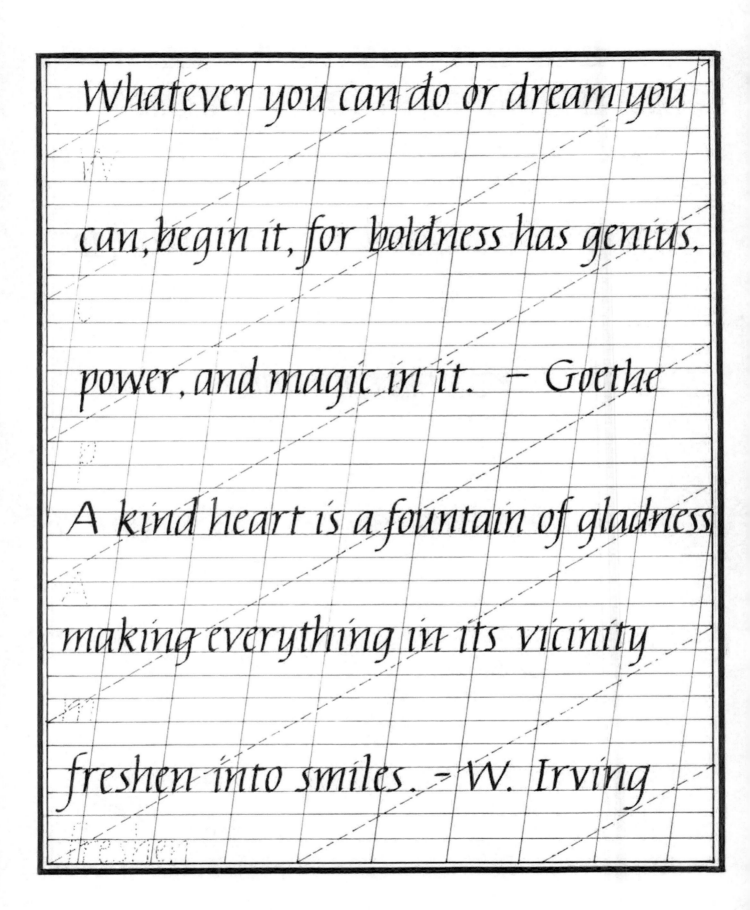

Whatever you can do or dream you

can, begin it, for boldness has genius,

power, and magic in it. — Goethe

A kind heart is a fountain of gladness

making everything in its vicinity

freshen into smiles. —W. Irving

202

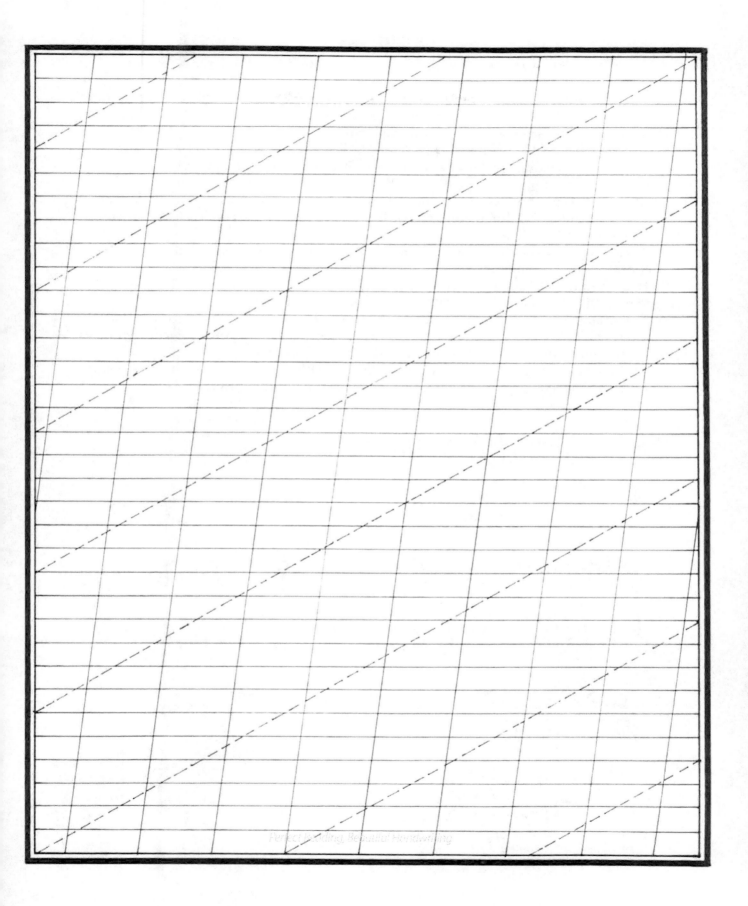

## Variations

Here are some of the many variations that you can do on the Italic small letters and capitals.

Notice that the basic shape of the letter does not usually change. What happens is that certain letters can naturally be extended, in order to make them look more "fancy" or beautiful. Use these extensions only if they truly make your writing more beautiful, but not if they make your writing harder to read. (If too many of these variations are used, writing may become crowded looking.) Horizontal extenders should only be used at the beginning or ending of a whole line of writing, never in the middle of a word or line of writing. The capitals on the facing page are only meant to be used to start off words, or for initials, but never for whole words. It is too hard to read whole words written in Swash capitals.

Trace and copy the variations on these pages and the quotations and names on the following pages. Then practice using these variations on your own.

It is also possible to write a fast version of Italic with the edged pen, and if you do this, you may wish to leave off the serifs and use the simpler letters.

Calligraphy simply means beautiful handwriting. There are different levels of skill that can be achieved in calligraphy, just as there are in music, sports, etc. Someday you may want to refine your skills and become a truly great calligrapher.

This book, however, will give you an excellent start in achieving beautiful handwriting for practical purposes, which will serve you well throughout your life.

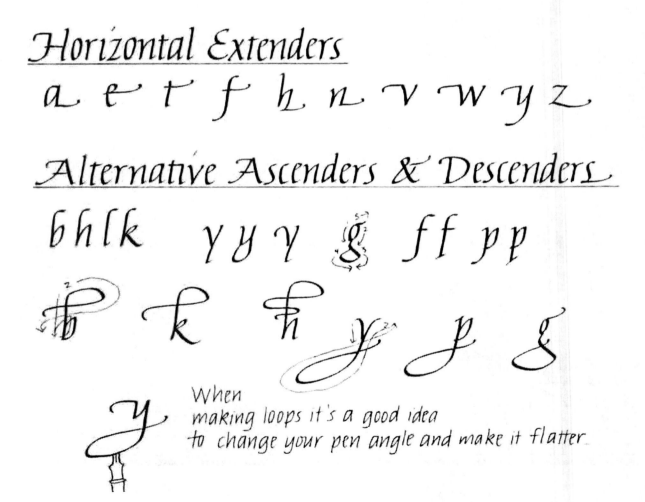

204

# Swash Capitals

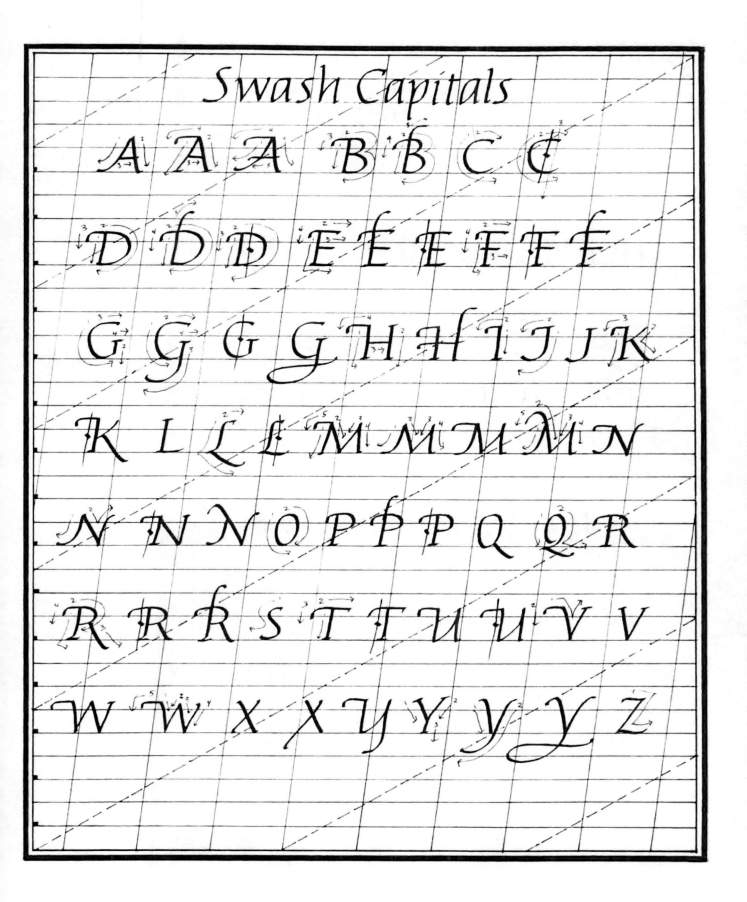

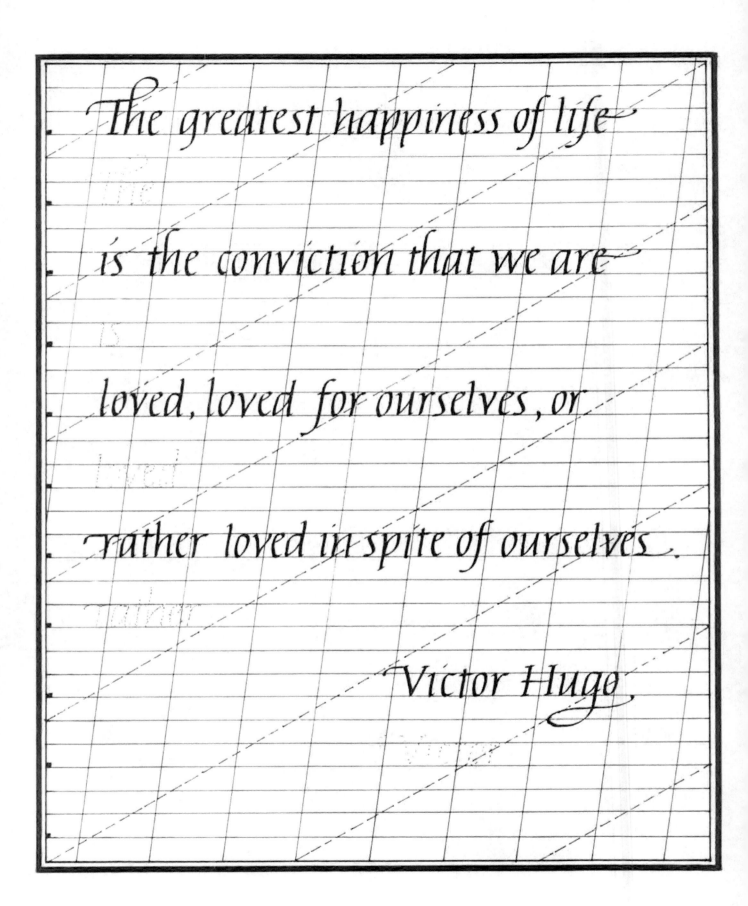

The greatest happiness of life
is the conviction that we are
loved, loved for ourselves, or
rather loved in spite of ourselves.

Victor Hugo

206

Amanda    Jennifer Nicola

Michael    Daniel    Christopher

Elizabeth    Caroline    Emily

Jamie    Ryan    Jonathan

Mellissa    Tiffany    Laura Sue

Janet Sarah Smith    Holly Jones

# Joined Writing with an Edged Pen

Trace and copy these quotations with an edged pen. Allow some joins to occur, for fast writing.

Live this day as if it were the last. Kerr

Let your life lightly dance on the edges of time

like dew on the tip of a leaf. — Tagore

The first great gift we can bestow on others

is a good example.    Morrell

It is well to read everything of something, and

everything of something.

( Done with an Osmiroid fine nib )

But words are things, and a small drop of ink,

Falling like dew, upon a thought, produces

That which, makes thousands, perhaps millions,

think ...     Lord Byron


A room without books is a body without a soul.

Marcus Tullius Cicero


A library of wisdom is more precious than all

wealth ...   Richard de Bury

Judge not, and you will not be judged;

condemn not, and you will not be

condemned. Forgive, and you will be

forgiven; give, and it will be given to you;

good measure, pressed down, shaken

together, running over, will be put into your

lap. For the measure you give will be the

measure you get back. Luke 6·37

( Done with an Osmiroid medium nib )

210

Love is patient and kind ; love is not jealous or boastful ; it is not arrogant or rude. Love does not insist on it's own way ; it is not irritable or resentful ; it does not rejoice at wrong, but rejoices in the right. Love bears all things, believes all things, hopes all things, endures all things.

1 Corinthians · 13

Dear Student,

Congratulations! You have now completed the Handwriting section of this book ... your Italic writing will have it's own unique look, since no two people do it exactly the same way.

Continue to experiment with different pens, letter variations, and writing speeds until you feel most comfortable.

Always try to leave big margins on the page around your writing. If you do, it will look more attractive and be easier to read as well.

May you have a lifetime filled with joy in writing! You can bring great joy to others with your beautiful writing as well. Everyone loves to receive letters and special cards, especially when they are beautiful to look at! So put your new skill to work ... spread light and love through your beautiful writing ...

Sincerely,
Caroline Adams

# RECOMMENDED BOOKS FOR PARENTS

Beck, Joan, *How to Raise a Brighter Child*, Simon & Schuster, 1986.

Dodson, Fitzhugh, *Give Your Child a Head Start in Reading*, Simon & Schuster 1986.

Flesch, Rudolf, *Why Johnny Can't Read*, Harper & Row, 1955, 1981.
   *Why Johnny Still Can't Read*, Harper & Row, 1981.

Hainstock, Elizabeth, *Teaching Montessori in the Home—The Preschool Years*, Random House, 1981.
   *Teaching Montessori in the Home—The School Years*, New American Library, 1971.

# SELECT BIBLIOGRAPHY

Becker, Paula, *How Johnny Can Read: A Time-Tested Method of Functional Phonics*, Falcon's Wing Press, 1957.

Chall, Jeanne, *Learning to Read: The Great Debate*, McGraw Hill, 1967.

Diehl, Kathryn, *Johnny Still Can't Read—But You Can Teach Him at Home*, Kathryn Diehl, 1976.

Fairbank, Alfred, *A Handwriting Manual*, Watson-Guptill, 1975.
   *Renaissance Handwriting*, World Publishing Co., 1960.
   *The Beacon Writing Books*, Ginn & Co., 1958.

Hay Julie, *Reading with Phonics*, Lippincott, 1968.

Henderson, Ellen, *Phonics in Learning to Read*, Exposition Press, 1967.

Knudsen Adams, Carolyn, *An Italic Calligraphy Handbook*, Stemmer House, 1985.

Malloy, Terry, *Montessori and Your Child*, Schocken Books, 1974.

Shattuck, Barbara, *Get Back to Phonics*, Step-by-Step Publications, 1985.

Stevenson, Nancy, *The Natural Way to Reading*, Little Brown & Co., 1974.

Wolf, Aline D., *Tutoring is Caring: You Can Help Someone to Learn to Read*, Montessori Learning Center, 1976.

## FOR ADDITIONAL INSTRUCTION

*Barchowsky Fluent Handwriting* — www.bfhhandwriting.com

*Teach Your Child to Read in 100 Easy Lessons* by Engelmann, Haddox, and Bruner

1857 McGuffey Readers with Instructions for Use with Charlotte Mason Methods — 1857McGuffey.com

## Other books from Everyday Education

### Excellence in Literature curriculum by Janice Campbell (Grades 8-12)
*Excellence in Literature helps you teach college prep classic literature and writing to your teen, even if you don't know Virginia Woolf from Beowulf!*

English I: *Introduction to Literature*
English II: *Literature and Composition*
English III: *American Literature*
English IV: *British Literature*
English V: *World Literature*
 —Complete Curriculum (all five years in a binder)
*Handbook for Writers* by Ian Johnston; Janice Campbell, ed.

### Language Arts
*Model-Based Writing: How to Use Writing Lessons that Work* by Janice Campbell (any age)
*Perfect Reading, Beautiful Handwriting* by Caroline Joy Adams
*The Elegant Essay* by Lesha Myers: Teacher's Manual and Student Book
— *Elegant Essay*: Student Book only
*Evaluate Writing the Easy Way* (Parent aid)
*Working it Out*: Poetry Analysis /Devotional with George Herbert

### 1857 McGuffey Readers
*First Eclectic Reader*
*Second Eclectic Reader*
*Third Eclectic Reader*
*Fourth Eclectic Reader*
*Fifth Eclectic Reader*
*Sixth Eclectic Reader*
— Set of Readers 1, 2, and 3
— Set of Readers 4, 5, and 6
— Set of all six Readers

### High School
*Transcripts Made Easy* by Janice Campbell
*Get a Jump Start on College*
*TimeFrame: The Twaddle-Free Timeline*
Microbusiness for Teens curriculum by Carol Topp, CPA — 4 books
Chenier's *Practical Math Dictionary* and *Application Guide* — Set of 2 books

You will find these resources, plus articles on how to teach with these books, at Everyday-Education. com. Even more articles are at Janice Campbell's blog, DoingWhatMatters.com.

Everyday Education, LLC, P.O. Box 549, Ashland, VA 23005
www.Everyday-Education.com
www.ExcellenceinLiterature.com • www.1857McGuffey.com

CPSIA information can be obtained
at www.ICGtesting.com
Printed in the USA
FFOW03n1421130916
27516FF